THE POWER OF
GRATITUDE

THE POWER OF
GRATITUDE

The thankful way to a happier, healthier you

Lois Blyth

CICO BOOKS
LONDON NEW YORK

Published in 2017 by CICO Books

An imprint of Ryland Peters & Small Ltd
20–21 Jockey's Fields   341 E 116th St
London WC1R 4BW   New York, NY 10029

www.rylandpeters.com

10 9 8 7 6 5 4 3 2 1

Text © Sarah Sutton 2017
Design and illustration © CICO Books 2017

A CIP catalog record for this book is available from
the Library of Congress and the British Library.

ISBN: 978-1-78249-439-3

Printed in China

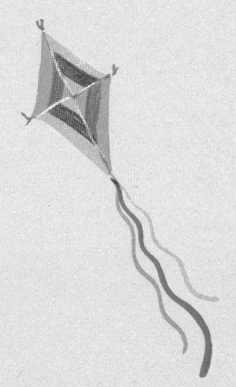

Editor: Rosie Lewis
Designer: Geoff Borin
Illustrator: Daniel Haskett

Commissioning editor: Kristine Pidkameny
Senior editor: Carmel Edmonds
Art director: Sally Powell
Production manager: Gordana Simakovic
Publishing manager: Penny Craig
Publisher: Cindy Richards

contents

introduction

living life with a grateful heart

There is much more to gratitude than giving, receiving, and saying thank you. It is a subtly positive way to gradually transform not only your world, but also the world of those around you—and, beyond that, the world we all live in. Gratitude can make great things happen because it has the capacity to open our hearts and show us the art of possibility. Feeling thankful is not always easy, but it offers a pathway to acceptance, in all its forms.

Whole-hearted gratitude is an uplifting, expansive, and positive way of being that leads to appreciation and times of fun and laughter. Sharing, caring, and togetherness are some of the essentials of being human. Feeling thankful makes us want to give back—to those who have helped us, cared for us, who love us—or who quite simply make us happy.

The magic happens when thoughts of gratitude are transformed into positive action. They become a gift of wholehearted appreciation that expands with further giving. Each time one person expresses gratitude to another, the feeling of being appreciated encourages both people to be more generous-spirited to others—and so it goes on.

Whether expressed in the warmth of kindness or friendship, the simplicity of a few written lines or a phone call, or the capacity to offer comfort to someone in pain, or symbolized in the form of a gift, gratitude is always about connection. It offers thanks with an awareness that life is not about "me," but about "us," and that relating to others offers greater joy than focusing on ourselves alone.

Gratitude may also offer comfort during times of grief and challenge. When we feel thankful, our perception shifts and the world becomes a place of greater optimism and hope. In remembering to value others for who they are or for what they bring to our lives, we are more likely to overlook or forgive those things that make us feel less than appreciative.

"Nothing is more honorable than the grateful heart."

Seneca (4 BCE–36 CE), Roman philosopher

Perhaps more than anything else, living life with gratitude can put us back in balance. It is a conscious pathway to fulfillment and contentment. Thinking of the bigger picture can be humbling. Taking time to recognize everything we can be thankful for offers relief from disenchantment and allows us the freedom to be ourselves.

Using this book

This book doesn't need to be read from cover to cover. It is designed to be dipped into—for reassurance, to help you regain perspective, or to prompt ideas for gifts or giving. It can be used as a source of daily wisdom or as an occasional guide.

CHAPTER 1

getting started

Saying "thank you" is common courtesy in every language—we all use this expression of gratitude every day. It is more than a polite habit of speech. When we focus on increasing our level of appreciation, we bring greater joy and enrichment to our lives.

The intention throughout this book is not to overwhelm you with things to do and rituals to keep to, but simply to invite you to dip in with an open mind to the possibilities that living with gratitude can offer.

seeing contrast

We are in the midst of a Gratitude Revolution! Everywhere, more people are giving more thanks, more often, and it is helping us to appreciate all that life has to offer. How can this be, when so many areas of the world are in turmoil? Does it offer us hope for the future?

Gratitude flourishes in situations of contrast, perhaps because that is when we can see most clearly how fortunate we are. When it is dark we appreciate the gift of light; when we are ill we appreciate good health; when we are lonely we appreciate our friends through their absence; when junk food is the only thing on the menu, we long for home cooking. So, too, when we are shocked by the horrors of war, we feel thankful for the safety of loved ones; when we see others struggle, we are more inclined to appreciate our own lives; when we are in despair, we move toward hope.

The beauty of a grateful attitude is that by focusing consciously on all we have to be grateful for, we create ever greater contrasts. We begin to see that the world we have created could become even better, and so we seek ways to make that change happen.

"When you rise in the morning, give thanks for the light, for your life, for your strength. Give thanks for your food and for the joy of living. If you see no reason to give thanks, the fault lies in yourself."

Tecumseh (1768–1813), Shawnee Chief

start where you are

Gratitude begins with a first step: giving thanks for big things, small things, and people who matter. As optimism grows, we develop confidence and increased will to make a difference—and gradually we influence those around us, too. The more frequently we step away from complacency and choose to move toward gratitude, the greater the possibility of diminishing indifference in our own lives and in the world around us.

Gratitude is not a destination; it is a state of mind and being. You can quite simply start where you are, right now, with three simple questions:

Who do I feel grateful to have in my life?

What has already happened today that I can be thankful for?

How shall I record this moment or show my appreciation?

Making a habit of answering these questions can quickly make your life happier and more contented. You will learn more about how to answer these questions in the pages that follow.

nurturing gratitude

From pagan times to the present day, the rhythm and language of the seasons have become embedded in our way of life. Spring, especially, is associated with new growth and new beginnings. It is the ideal time to clear your mind and consciously get rid of unhelpful attitudes that are no longer serving your needs, to make space for the new attitude in residence: Gratitude.

Gratitude, like all newly planted seeds, needs patience, warmth, and nurture to allow it to grow and to give it the space and time to shine. It may be sensitive in the early stages of growth and easily suffocated by darker feelings of bitterness, anger, resentment,

and jealousy, which absorb too much energy. By staying attentive and weeding out unhelpful attitudes, you can allow gratitude and thankfulness to burgeon.

Companionship, friendship, shared laughter, and kindness help gratitude to develop unabated. Regular feeding with appreciation, understanding, and courtesy also works wonders. But beware of doubt, suspicion, and cynicism; they are common pests that undermine sincerity. The moment any kind of ulterior motive is suspected, genuine thankfulness falters and finds it harder to thrive. With regular nurture, gratitude will flower into optimism and positivity that sustain health and well-being for life.

why giving thanks matters

We all need gratitude. We need to receive it so that we feel appreciated, and we need to extend it to others and to the world we are part of, to stay connected and appreciative of what we have.

Material possessions do not necessarily make us feel happier. How can we be gratefully satisfied with what we already have if we are always looking for something newer or better? There can be a tendency to feel less contented the more we own—because the more we have, the more we want. Tuning in to gratitude helps us to stay grounded. It is not about accepting the status quo, but about regaining perspective and appreciating all that is good about where we are and what we have right now.

GRATITUDE IN PRACTICE:

Living life with conscious gratitude

In her book *Fragile Mystics* (2015), Rev. Magdalen Smith introduces us to Rosie Pinto de Carvalho, who tells her: "I don't have everything I love, but I love everything I have." Rosie lives in a favela in one of the poorest areas of Rio de Janeiro, Brazil. What an inspiring attitude to life! In that single comment, Rosie reinforces awareness that there is very little connection between material possessions and contentment. The less we own, the more we appreciate and treasure what our belongings represent.

a gift to yourself

"Preserve your memories, keep them well."

Louisa May Alcott (1832–1888), writer

An attitude of gratitude gains strength the more we practice it. Making simple changes to the way we view the world each day gradually adjusts our perspective, almost without us noticing. So this section is all about you—and for you. It begins with a carefully chosen gift to yourself: your gratitude journal, app, or diary.

Give your choice of journal some thought before you embark on your mission of gratitude, because it needs to become a joy to use. I was very lucky that a dear friend had given me a beautiful notebook that had been waiting two years for the right moment to be used. It was exactly the right size, shape, and quality to inspire me—but I am an old-fashioned pen-and-paper person. If you are likely to share some key moments on Twitter or Pinterest, you may prefer to use your cell phone or a specially designed app to record your moments of gratitude. Do remember that your journal is intended for you personally, rather than your community of friends, as some comments may be quite private. You may wish to be selective about what you share more broadly so that you don't find yourself restraining your thoughts in your daily journal for fear of what others will think.

beginning your journal

As you complete your journal, it will become a resource to treasure, that will reflect your thoughts and your progress back to you over time. There are many books and resources on journaling, and the pages that follow include a few guidelines that will help you to decide when and how keeping a journal will work for you.

First a little note of what your journal is not: It is not a shopping list, nor a "to do" list, nor a diary of events. It is, however, a place

where you can express yourself freely and reflect not only on the things you feel grateful for, but also on ways you can turn negative reactions into something more positive. Over time, it will become a dossier of appreciation, a cluster of precious moments that connect you to the people in your life, to the world and all the good things in it.

Getting started is the easy bit: keeping going can be tougher. If completing the journal every day becomes a chore, and you find yourself laden with feelings of guilt because you have missed a day, a week, or more, then try gathering your thoughts in a way that has more meaning for you. Instead of words, use pictures, mind maps, doodles, or a combination of some or all of these if it helps you to do it more often. There are no fixed rules of expression.

A word to the wise, however: there are many behavioral experts who recommend that focusing on changing behavior consistently, for a minimum period of 21 days, is necessary for a lasting effect. The 21-day rule is said to work because you are

Remember the 21-day rule

training your brain to think in a different way. In effect, you are sending a message via your neural pathways that shouts: "Thought diversion: this way to positivity!" So it is worth persevering.

Gratitude does not exist only in the current moment. Reviewing times of thankfulness and gratitude for past events can offer great comfort at any time, as well as helping us to adjust and broaden our perspective.

getting out of your own way

You may find yourself feeling skeptical about starting a gratitude journal. "What is the point? What a cliché. What good will it do? I haven't got time..." There are many reasons why we might tell ourselves that there is no point in giving the process a try. If you find yourself feeling resistant to the idea, perhaps pause to ask yourself: What have I got to lose?

As someone who was initially doubtful that my journal would be much more than a list of "thank yous," I was amazed at how quickly and how profoundly the process affected the way I viewed my experiences. Because the journal is intended only for positive thoughts, it forces the writer to find a way to reframe everyday happenings. The scientists are right. By deliberately choosing a positive outlook we do gradually alter the way we think—about ourselves and about the events that happen to us and around us. Expressing gratitude in a conscious way encourages us to adopt a new attitude, tweaking word choices and thought processes to open the heart and change the way we view the world.

In reality, it is impossible to hold every moment of gratitude in your memory, not even those that seem indelibly printed on your heart. Capturing passing moments in your journal is the equivalent of creating a personal album that you can look through for reinforcement and treasure forever. It frees your mind to tune in to other things, as well. It becomes self-perpetuating and takes the mind beyond itself, to the bigger picture.

why do we find it so hard to do simple things that are good for us?

Some people who begin their gratitude journal with enthusiasm may abandon the idea before it becomes a habit. Maybe positive thoughts begin to flow more easily and it feels unnecessary to write them down; or perhaps, after a long day, it feels "too much" to spend time gathering your thoughts.

When negativity becomes the dominant state of mind, positivity becomes irritating and feels irrelevant. Grumbling can become a verbal comfort blanket that provides an illusion of control. When life is tough, anger and tiredness can get in the way of self-care. In such moments we may need to adopt a conscious change of mind to adjust our direction and chart a course back toward gratitude—one thought at a time.

The six As of thankfulness:

Choose your **Attitude**—Finding ways to develop a consciously positive outlook is an integral part of becoming "thank full."

Increase **Awareness**—Tuning in to your environment and the events of each day increases consciousness.

Appreciate the everyday—Finding joy in small things expands our appreciation of the bigger things, too.

Allocate time—If you are writing a journal, it can be helpful to do it at the same time each day, so that you begin to remember automatically.

Remain **Authentic**—Everyone has their own style of behavior and of expression. Stay true to yourself.

Acceptance—The most important "A" of all. Gratitude is at its most powerful when you allow others to give, and can accept wholeheartedly.

what should I write about?

The easy answer is anything and everything—or anyone—that holds meaning for you and has an impact on your life, whether now or in the past. You might feel thankful for something that you have experienced personally, or grateful for something that has happened to someone else. It could be something as simple as hearing a great new track on the radio or buying a new sweater, or as profound as being reunited with a friend, or hearing news of a neighbor who is recovering from illness.

People: your friends, family, neighbors, colleagues, kind strangers, teachers, past acquaintances, anyone who has inspired you. What kindnesses have you experienced recently? Whom are you grateful to have in your life? Who has offered you their trust or loyalty? Who has supported and helped you? Whom would you like to thank for past generosity or wisdom?

Places: home and what it means to you, vacation places that trigger wonderful memories, places of interest that inspire you, destinations that feed your imagination and dreams for the future.

Heritage: where you came from, your culture, traditions, and history.

Things: wonderful objects, clever design, amazing architecture: the joy of driving your car, enjoying a great movie or TV series, the comfort of your favorite chair after spending time away.

The natural world: the sky, sea, animals, birds, trees, plants, the weather, and landscape offer so much that inspires us and that we can be grateful for.

You: your uniqueness, your talents, foibles, friends, successes and failures, goals and achievements. When we live more consciously and more gratefully, we become more alive and alert to the potential of each moment.

Changing perspective

Oprah Winfrey is well known for her actively positive attitude to life, and she has spoken about the importance of her gratitude journal. Interestingly, she has also written about the impact of being too busy to keep up her journal. After a particularly busy period when she was feeling less joy in her work, she took time to look back at a journal entry from a year or two earlier and noticed how much more contented she had been then. She realized on reflection that she had been no less busy during that year—she had simply been more disciplined about making time to reflect each day on the good things that had happened. When she took time to look for reasons to feel grateful, "something always showed up."

how much should I write?

There are no rules. It is up to you how much you write—and this will differ from day to day. For some people, writing a simple statement will be enough; for others, greater detail will come naturally and will be helpful. Many people find that they start with a few basic bullet points, but before long they want to write more. There is no need to force the process. As you develop the gratitude habit, you will find your own pattern.

the power of three

Your journal can include as many ways to say "thank you" as you wish—but there seems to be magic in the power of three. Three offers stability and balance: it is the base of the triangle, the third leg of the stool. Time is spoken about in divisions of three: past, present, and future. It is common to say that things happen in threes. Your day is made up of morning, afternoon, and evening. Spiritually, the number three has great significance.

Remember
the power of
3

Most of us can think of three things to be grateful for each day:

• How lucky that the sun shone all day today.

• The roses are looking fabulous and they smell astonishing.

• It was great to bump into my friend and I am so glad we have finally arranged a date to meet.

Staying tuned in to the things that happen around you has great power in its simplicity and will increase in impact over time. You may find that your journal evolves a little like this:

1. One note of appreciation for a kindness.

2. One observation about the world around you.

3. One deeper thought.

Martin Seligman (see page 53) recommends thinking of "three good things" about each day. He has proven that this simple action leads directly to an increase in well-being. You could try it for yourself. It is as simple as:

1.
_____

_____

2.
_____

_____

3.
_____

_____

As you develop the gratitude habit, you will discover that you go to greater depths with your thoughts. You may want to write more expressively about what the pathway to gratitude has shown you— and how it is transforming your thinking.

1. It was lovely of Jo to insist on picking me up when my car broke down earlier.

2. If I hadn't broken down I wouldn't have had the chance to spend so much time chatting with her and her daughter.

3. I am so relieved that the car broke down today and not on the way to work on Monday. It is interesting how often something good comes out of something annoying.

1. I am grateful to Mike for taking the dogs for a walk after school.

2. What a joy it is to live so near a park where the dogs can run freely!

3. The trees look really beautiful at the moment. They are such a precious resource.

writing is not for me—what are the alternatives?

There are as many ways to express our thoughts of gratitude as there are ways to express ourselves: photography, music, painting, doodling, and the spoken word all have power. You may simply want to collect some symbols of gratitude: a pebble from a beach, a concert ticket, a greetings card, or a letter.

The benefit of recording something in a permanent form is that it increases in depth and momentum over time—and it is always there to refer to. However, the essence of gratitude is that it has the capacity to become a powerful force for change and optimism, whether it is expressed occasionally or every moment of every day.

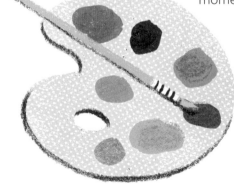

how do I turn a negative into a positive?

Turning bad into good is not always easy or possible—
especially in the short term—but it can definitely help
to look consciously at the brighter side of a situation.
(See Chapter 4 for more about this.) If you've had
one of those days, and everything seems to have gone
wrong, it can be hard to know what to write in your
gratitude journal. Instead of focusing on the bad things, spend
some time thinking about what else happened to you, however
insignificant. You might be surprised! Gratitude has the capacity to
improve our sense of well-being and optimism, which can gradually
help us to let go of or make sense of negative feelings or memories.

Looking on the bright side:

"Although I am terrified by the idea of the medical treatment, I am
hugely relieved that I now know what is wrong with me—and the
medical team are being wonderful. I am starting to allow myself to
hope that I can get through this."

Being completely honest with yourself:

"Although I am devastated that I have been made redundant, and
I am still very worried about the future, I must admit that I had been
thinking of leaving that job for a while, and perhaps this period may
give me time to retrain."

Acknowledging the dark side:

"Although this is a disruptive time, I feel grateful for the memory of
the arguments we had because it helps me to know in my heart that
it is better that we have parted."

However, there is one context in which gratitude is not the answer to
the immediate situation. Gratitude does not thrive in a situation of
servitude or beholdenness. There are some circumstances where the
right thing to do is not to accept or feel grateful for your situation—
and instead to feel thankful that you have free will to bring about
change, with the help of others, too, as necessary.

gratitude in action

You can start to put gratitude into action right now, simply with a positive approach and an open heart. However, living with gratitude may be more powerful if practical tweaks and changes are made to the home and work environment, too.

creating a sacred space

Is there an area in your home where you can feel at peace? For some it will be a whole room, for others it may be a particular chair, or a spot by a window or outside in the garden.

This can become a sacred space for contemplation. If you feel anxious about the sense of ritual involved, be reassured that there is no need for any kind of faith or conscious belief for this process to be helpful. Making space within your world for a positive nook that

GRATITUDE IN PRACTICE:

The bigger picture

"I had become fed up with certain aspects of my job," says Grace, "and was thinking of leaving. I was having trouble thinking of anything positive to write in my gratitude journal, too, so I flicked back through it, partly for inspiration. I came across a couple of entries that described how grateful I felt to get the job in the first place! That helped me to think about the bigger picture and things I can do to bring about changes in my place of work instead, rather than leaving and causing upheaval."

you automatically associate with feelings of wholehearted thanks can trigger wonderful feelings of peace and acceptance.

A sense of calm is essential for replenishing feelings of gratitude, especially after a taxing or tiring day. Creating an area for contemplation can help you to feel more connected, focused, and grounded. Just as you would clear your work surfaces before preparing to cook or create something, so too it makes sense to clear your mind before focusing on all there is to feel grateful for.

creating a gratitude altar

Altars have played an important part in rites and rituals of thanksgiving since prehistoric times, as well as being an anchor point for receiving the sacrament in Western religions. They cross cultures and are often mobile, too. Armies use the drum as an altar in the battlefield (and still hold drumhead services to this day), and spiritual leaders around the world carry simple symbols of prayer with them at all times, in case of need.

Just as we may light a candle in remembrance or as a sign of peace, or display objects on a desk or mantelpiece to remind us of important moments in our lives, so an altar provides a surface where we can focus our attention and change our thought processes for a moment.

Creating an altar is very personal. If you feel moved to make one in your home, think about whether you want it to be in a place that is light and bright in the morning; or cozy and softly lit for use in the evenings. Do you want to be able to hear sounds of birdsong outside your window, or do you want silence or music so that you can shut out the world? You may like to include:

• Candles—scented or unscented

• Flowers

• Natural elements, such as pebbles, shells, and/or leaves

• Symbols that have personal meaning for you, such as a ring, crystals, or a sacred object

Altars provide a focus for offering thanks for all that life provides. Put to one side any doubts and preconceptions you may have about whether this will work, and allow yourself the time to create a beautiful space that makes you want to give from your heart, and open yourself up to greater understanding. (Note: If the word "altar" has serious religious significance for you, and you feel uncomfortable with the secular use, think of it simply as a table or platform where you can focus your attention on the power of gratitude.)

There are no rules about how you should express or focus on giving thanks. This is your personal route to experiencing gratitude, and no one else's.

making time for gratitude

Gratitude is a gift that you offer to yourself, and others—
and beyond.

grateful meditation

In many spiritual practices prayer and meditation begin with the
offering of thanks to the elders and ancestors whose lives and
challenges have contributed to who we are today.

In a whole-life meditation you might want to begin with the
day you were born, and work through each year of your life to
acknowledge important people and places, things that have
happened and those whom you appreciate.

The greatest value at first, however, is in focusing on the here and
now. Take the time to focus, ideally in a place where you will not be
disturbed. This might be at home, or in a park, or quietly on a train,
while walking, or while traveling.

Allow your body to relax, from your toes to the top of your head.
Pay special attention to letting go of the tension in different areas
of your body, such as your feet, knees, shoulders, or jawline, by
stretching, moving your body, or even yawning.

Be aware of whether you are starting from a mood of anger,
frustration, or sadness—or whether you are already feeling positive
and full of gratitude. Don't judge yourself for your feelings, or try to
change them; just be aware of your state of mind.

Now breathe easily and naturally. Be patient with yourself, and
begin to observe and recollect. Consider whom or what you are
thankful for, and why.

Depending on your state of mind, it may help to focus on a few
details:

• The dawn chorus that I heard this morning.

• My warm gratitude toward the young boy who helped me yesterday.

- The bright yellow of the daffodils that are coming into flower.
- The amazing full moon in such a beautifully clear sky the other evening.

Simply noticing and appreciating the positive elements of the world around you will have an uplifting effect. Starting off with small things leads quickly to thoughts of the big things:

- The love of my family.
- The kindness of my friends.
- The joy of watching my team score at the weekend.
- My relative health and the use of my body.
- The financial security that my job offers me.
- The memory of my mother's light and wisdom.

If you become distracted, watch where your attention goes. Don't fight your thoughts, but see whether you can reframe them with gratitude. For example, if someone has been annoying you: "I am grateful for having X as my friend, even though he has been driving me insane lately. I know he has been going through a hard time. I will give him a call."

When I discussed this process with a friend of mine, she was confused about what or whom the gratitude was being directed at. She was wary of and uncomfortable with the uncertainty of abstract concepts such as thanking the universe. It really doesn't matter whom you thank, or how you do it. As the research evidence in the following chapter shows, the person who will benefit most from your feelings of gratitude is you. However, when we value the wonder of the universe as a whole it becomes much harder to feel upset about life's smaller irritations. From such a great height we can no longer see them, or feel them as acutely—and eventually they may even cease to matter.

CHAPTER 2

gratitude is good for us

Scientific research is gradually building a body of evidence that supports what we have always known instinctively—that gratitude is good for our health. It shows up not only in the way we look after our physical fitness and nutritional health, but also in our mental well-being and lifestyle choices. Gratitude helps us to develop an optimistic outlook and plays an important role in how we feel about our life, work, and purpose.

We experience the impact of gratitude not only directly, through the impact on our health and well-being, but also indirectly, through the power of positive thinking and feelings of self-worth. Feeling gratitude for our work and fully embracing the varied roles we have in life helps to generate a sense of completeness—and of thankfulness for this life, right here, right now.

the healing power of gratitude

Health experts and researchers around the world are starting to pay greater attention to gratitude and its impact on our health, thought processes, and behavior. From the Greater Good Science Center in Berkeley, California, to the University of Birmingham, England (in association with the John Templeton Foundation), scientists are measuring and assessing what makes us grateful and what happens when we are grateful. Early indications are that it is good for the heart as well as the soul.

In 2015, the *Journal of Happiness Studies* (yes, there really is such a publication!) reported on a short-term study in the United States that compared the benefits to patients of keeping a) a gratitude journal; b) a kindness journal; and c) no journal over a period of 14 days, while they were waiting to be referred to a counselor. Interestingly, the only group that felt any benefit during such a short period of time was the one that focused on gratitude.

In another project, demonstrated in a video on Curt Rosengren's Ripple Revolution website, a group of volunteers were asked to complete a happiness questionnaire. They were then asked to identify someone who had had an important impact on their lives, and to

> *"Let us be thankful to people who make us happy; they are the gardeners who make us blossom."*
>
> Marcel Proust (1871–1922), writer

whom they had reason to feel very grateful. Each person was then asked to write an expression of thanks to that individual, in the form of a letter. It was an intense exercise for all involved, and everyone assumed that once they had completed the assignment, that would be the end of the session. Far from it, however. Each participant was asked to telephone the person they wished to thank, there and then—and to read out to them the letter they had written.

The effect was extraordinary. Quite apart from the emotional impact on the person who received the unexpected expression of heartfelt gratitude at the other end of the phone line, there was a measurable and positive outcome for the person who was offering their thanks, too. When the volunteers retook the questionnaire, their scores increased by an average of 90 percent! (In contrast, those who had written letters but had not phoned scored an increase of 20 percent. Still extremely positive—but not as remarkable.) It seems that gratitude is a very fast-acting emotion, and one that has an immediate impact on our well-being.

What does a grateful brain look like?

Researchers have found that when people express gratitude, their brains show increased levels of activity in the anterior cingulate cortex and the medial prefrontal cortex. Both areas are associated with the way we process emotions and express empathy, our bonds with others, and moral judgment.

your gratitude power pack

Gratitude is like a battery: it must be kept fully charged to function at optimum power.

Everyone feels down from time to time, for all kinds of reasons. We are human, after all. However, if the habits of negativity, blaming, and moaning have crept into your life, you are gradually wearing yourself out—and may be having a negative impact on those around you, too. Like a battery, if you let your sense of appreciation run on empty for too long, it will take longer to re-energize.

The good news is that it is far easier to recharge your gratitude power pack than it is to charge a battery. During more wobbly or uncertain times, consciously cultivating an attitude of gratitude can be extremely helpful.

choose your words with care

The enemies of gratitude are negative thoughts, which influence our choice of words and then our actions. Pay attention to how you react and the words you use when faced with disappointment, or when things don't quite go to plan. Our use of language tells us a great deal about our state of mind: "I wish," "I regret," "If only," "I should have," "I wanted to," "I am fed up," "Why should I," "I can't … "

Oh, the joy of "shouldawouldacoulda." All these phrases are energy depleters that take away our personal power and deplete our positivity. Over time, as we blame other people or bad luck for our circumstances, we begin to feel powerless over our own lives. It may become harder to feel joy or to act spontaneously, and difficult to forgive those around us for being less than perfect, or the world for not living up to our expectations. The natural power of gratitude, however, is such that it is also quite easy to adjust our responses and reframe our experience in a more positive light, if we choose to do so.

the language of gratitude

By contrast with complaints and regrets, the language of gratitude has a feel-good factor that tends to be infectious and lifts others, too. Giving positive voice to your feelings gives them additional power, although it can be challenging and emotional on occasion.

Make it a habit to say "thank you" for the simple things as well as the big things in life. You will be amazed at how much gratitude and appreciation you get back spontaneously in return.

Gratitude is a gift that reciprocates in goodwill. You will always get back as much as or more than you give—and your positivity and appreciative attitude will subtly influence others to become more positive, without anyone realizing it.

Try thinking to yourself, or writing down, or saying out loud in a private moment each day:

I am thankful for...

I am grateful for...

I am glad that...

I appreciate...

How kind that...

I offer gratitude for...

There's a donkey in here somewhere!

The story goes that a mother once took her two sons to a psychiatrist. One boy was very pessimistic and the other very optimistic, and she wanted to understand why they were so different. The psychiatrist put the pessimistic boy in a room with some new toys, in the hope that they would make him feel happy. The optimistic boy, meanwhile, was put in a room filled with dung, to see whether that would curb his optimism. The psychiatrist then began to observe their reactions.

The boy with the new toys was not happy at all. Instead of welcoming the gifts, he feared that if he played with them he would break something and everything would be ruined. The psychiatrist then looked in on the boy with the pile of dung. He had found a shovel and was happily digging away with great energy. "What are you doing?" the psychiatrist asked.

"I am trying to find the donkey," answered the boy.

"What makes you think there is a donkey?" asked the psychiatrist.

"Well," said the boy, *"with all this dung about, there must be one in here somewhere!"*

The tale is of course apocryphal. It is very unlikely that any self-respecting doctor would put a child in a room with a pile of dung! However, the message is clear: optimism is good for us. It helps us to be grateful for what we have, and encourages us to see opportunities where a pessimist may see an obstacle. Gratitude helps us to dig deep and find the positivity to overcome adversity in the most unlikely situations.

gratitude guru: **Eleanor H. Porter**

"There is something about everything that you can be glad about, if you keep hunting long enough to find it."

Eleanor H. Porter (1868–1920), *Pollyanna*

The original gratitude guru must be Pollyanna, a fictional character in the American classic children's story of the same name by Eleanor H. Porter. Unfailingly (and, some would say, unrelentingly) positive and cheery, Pollyanna is taught by her father to look for the good in everything and to be "glad" for every obstacle she faces in life, because something positive will be revealed in every situation. When she is sent to live with her strict and emotionally absent Aunt Polly after her father dies, she focuses on playing "the glad game" in the face of many trials and tribulations. In classic Hollywood style, her positive outlook eventually melts every heart. The Pollyanna stories became known as "The Glad Books," and the name Pollyanna is now synonymous with an extreme kind of naïve and boundless positivity.

The first Pollyanna story is unsettling by modern standards, even if the eventual outcome is positive. Pollyanna's cloak of gratitude protects her from the awareness that she is being deliberately and cruelly starved of care and affection by her aunt. However, the moral of the tale is very clear: even in adversity, when we have lost everything, living life with a glad heart and gratitude can help us to retain a sense of self-determination and optimism about the future. Eleanor Porter would have a lot in common with the positive psychology movement if she were alive today.

The Pollyanna factor

On a scale of 1 to 10, what is your Pollyanna-style "Gladness" score?

1   **2**   **3**   **4**   **5**   **6**   **7**   **8**   **9**   **10**

Grumbling Aunt Polly   Gladly Pollyanna

Are you somewhere between 5 and 10? Are you Pollyanna—a fully paid-up optimist, glad to be alive and grateful for everything that happens to you? Do you more often find yourself at the lower end of the scale—more Aunt Polly than Pollyanna? (See also the quiz on pages 136–137.)

Most of us are in the middle, around 5 or 6: full of enthusiasm one minute and easily let down the next; programmed to believe that everything will get better, but not beyond moaning a great deal when things don't work out as planned.

the abc of optimism

Gratitude is a nourishing force that helps us to develop optimism and appreciation. The moment we say thank you or consciously show appreciation, negativity diminishes. However, it is hard to change our instinctive behavior after the event. If we want to alter the way we react to situations and become more grateful, we must consciously change the way we think before and during an event or occurrence. Think about it as the **A**, **B**, **C** of optimism:

A is the trigger for the negative thoughts.
B is the behavior that has become an automatic response to that thought.
C is the consequence.

For example:

Each time your friend turns up late (**A**—the trigger) you start to feel resentment (**B**—the behavior). Rather than saying how you really feel, you say something sarcastic, which leads to an argument—which somehow turns out to be your fault (**C**—the consequence).

If, however, you know that her lateness will lead to you feeling resentful, you can be on the alert before **A** takes place, and prepare an alternative strategy.

For example, you could say: "Shall we meet an hour later, as I know you find it hard to get here promptly from work?" Or, if you are feeling braver, "I need to let you know that when you turn up late every time I take it personally, and it feels as if you don't respect my feelings, which is why I get upset."

Breaking the cycle breaks the negativity, and feeds an optimistic outlook instead.

gratitude in partnership

Many people feel they are living life in the fast lane, with insufficient time to "stop and stare." When we rush, we prevent ourselves from having the time to fully appreciate all that we are experiencing. There is a danger that we can become victims of circumstance rather than living consciously.

Sometimes we need time to understand the gift we have been given or to grasp the true impact of what is happening in life. Developing patience can allow time to refocus, or to see that there is benefit even in adverse experiences. Living life more slowly and taking time to notice how we are feeling increases our sense of awareness in the broadest sense. We start to pay greater attention and can choose to develop a sense of gratitude for other people and for our world.

The role of patience

The ability to delay gratification in childhood has long been associated with a greater capacity for material success in later life. However, factors that are allied with this are patience and gratitude.

In a study in the United States, participants were given the choice between receiving an immediate cash reward or waiting up to 12 months for a larger windfall of as much as $100. It turned out that those who showed the least patience and gratitude tended to claim payment at the $18 mark. The more grateful people held out, on average, until the amount reached $30.

The conclusion was that when we feel thankful for what we already have, we are less likely to be impatient in our responses and give in to the impulse for immediate gratification. (This sounds like a conclusion that is good for relationships, too!)

when gratitude doesn't work

"The harder we try with the conscious will to do something, the less we shall succeed."

Aldous Huxley (1894–1963), writer and philosopher

There is one negative trait that can become associated with the habit of gratitude: some people have the potential to develop a false sense of reality. This can take the form of an extreme and rather fatalistic belief that life is so positive that everything will be okay, whatever the evidence to the contrary. This can lead to problems such as ignoring bills, not going to the doctor, not acknowledging that something needs to be repaired. Gratitude does not absolve us from responsibility; it is more about achieving balance—appreciating that life is about giving and receiving rather than expecting and taking.

There are times, too, when we just don't want to take the trouble to feel consciously thankful—and moments when it can be incredibly irritating to be confronted with a "Pollyanna" approach to life. Full-on, upbeat optimism is not always appropriate, and a healthy dose of cynicism or humor can be equally beneficial.

According to Professor Julie Norem of Wellesley College in Massachusetts, a forced state of optimism and gratitude can make some people extremely anxious. She calls this "defensive pessimism." An over-emphasis on positive thinking can lead to a worrying sense of uncertainty because it creates a false sense of reality. This is where Authenticity comes in, from the six As of thankfulness on page 16. If you are having a rotten day, it is normal to feel low, and gratitude may not come naturally. Trying to force yourself to believe that something bad is actually good can be both unhealthy and distressing. There are times when patience is the key to gratitude, since the positive side of a situation may not be immediately apparent.

Remember to be *Authentic*

There is nothing wrong, then, with self-doubt or struggling to think positively. Plenty of people start from the premise that only by imagining the worst that can happen can they be reasonably sure that they will not be disappointed, whatever the outcome. Then there is plenty to be grateful for when they are proved right!

GRATITUDE IN PRACTICE:

Taking time to feel grateful

"I became very interested in practicing positivity in a conscious way after a particularly difficult time in my life," says Gina. "I have been told that I am a bit of an 'Eeyore' in my approach to things, and I worry a great deal. I wanted to see whether consciously changing my thoughts would make a permanent difference. However, after an enthusiastic beginning I found that I began to feel guilty if I did not feel grateful straight away. Many of the self-help books made me feel worse instead of better—as if I was doing something wrong. Living with gratitude is not a simple matter of saying that 'the world is alright' and then it shall be so. Some serious work has to be done along the way to consciously change one's thoughts and approach. These days I take my time to feel grateful. I aim to reframe things in a more positive light."

gratitude in action

There are many ways that you can show appreciation for the gift of your health and your body. It may sound obvious, but the key to success is to do things that you are drawn toward and that you enjoy. Here are a few ideas.

be grateful for your body

How many hours, days, or weeks have we all spent regretting that our bodies have some perceived flaw? The physical frame that you call a body carries you, enables you to breathe, and keeps your heart beating, even—within limits—when it is mistreated with the wrong kind of food, unhealthy behavior, or negative thoughts.

It may be time to show gratitude for your physical self by giving your body more of what it really needs to flourish and maintain good health. Take the pledge to give thanks for your body every day!

List three things that you like about your body and would like to give thanks for.

Remember:

1. One note of appreciation

2. One observation

3. One deeper thought

1. _____

_____

2. _____

_____

3. _____

_____

conscious nourishment

Nourishing your body in a healthy and thankful way begins with the shopping list, carries on with your chosen route around the store (we all know which aisles we should feel less grateful for!), and ends up at the checkout.

As anyone who has ever consciously changed their eating habits will know, the key to eating healthily is forward planning. Some people find that focusing anew on the beauty and color of fresh vegetables and thinking consciously about the goodness and nutrients can help them to drop the chocolate and swap saturated fats for healthy options. The majority of us, however, often struggle with following the healthy path, especially when under pressure.

• Feel grateful for the foods you enjoy that are healthy, and eat more of them. For example, if you enjoy the sweetness of nectarines, apples, bananas, or other fruits and juices, it can be helpful to have some on standby to distract your taste buds before you head off to the store.

• Feel thankful that sometimes, when we think we are hungry, we are simply bored, anxious, or thirsty. Try having a savory or hot drink, phoning a friend, or doing something that is active and different for a few minutes, and wait for the craving to pass.

• Feel delighted that our bodies prefer to heal and get well if they can. If you focus on swapping unhealthy patterns for healthy ones, it will get easier to maintain your new lifestyle. The chances are that your friends and family will notice the difference before you do.

• Finally, "think gratitude" for your new plan of action as you enter each store. That way, you will be less likely to overspend or to buy food that is less nourishing and that you will feel less grateful for later.

give back to your body

If you have been neglecting exercise and need to get started again, you may like to consider one or more of the following to begin with:

• Go for a meaningful walk each day—around the block, to a nearby park, or to somewhere new. (Borrow a friend's dog if that will help to motivate you!). Notice how your body feels as you breathe in the air and feel the wind on your skin. Realize that you really are miraculous—and that is worth being grateful for.

• Music is one of the most incredible gifts of all. Our bodies are designed for movement, so who can resist getting up to dance when the sound matches our mood? Dancing is exercise and pure enjoyment rolled into one. Whether dancing in the kitchen to the radio, or letting go in full party mode, dancing "gives back" to your body while music feeds your soul—the perfect way to feel thankful for being alive.

• Treat yourself to an occasional massage or reflexology session. In the right hands a treatment will help to balance your body and get rid of tension, so that your blood flows more readily, your gut works more healthily, and you feel revitalized. Feel gratitude for the expertise of the professional who gives you your treatment, and appreciate consciously how much better you are afterward.

• If you have access to a garden, spending 20 minutes or so a day weeding, planting, and nurturing will reap great rewards— for you as well as the plants. Take time to see what is growing, how things have changed since yesterday, the shapes, colors, scents, and behavior of every small thing, from an opening flower to the buzzing circuit of a bee.

• If you feel more adventurous, offering gratitude to others by taking part in a sponsored walk, half-marathon, or other challenge for a greater cause can help to get you focused, motivated, and fit at the same time.

making time for gratitude

We all lead busy lives, so "making time" for additional activities is not always an option. The beauty of living life more thankfully is that small changes in everyday thoughts and outlook can reap big rewards—with no need to find "extra" time in your daily routine.

the power of thank you

It is all too easy to take those whom we love and who care for us for granted. Saying "thank you" regularly to members of your family for everyday things has been shown to strengthen bonds and help to increase the sense of connection and togetherness.

getting from A to B

Daily commuters are masters at "going inwards" to create some mental space between themselves and their fellow travelers. Many wear headphones or focus on their cell phones or tablets. The journey to work is a natural time to start to "think more thankfully." Stuck in traffic? Squashed on the subway? Missed the bus? Late for work? Once you have accepted that you can do nothing about the situation, there is scope to divert your attention away from feeling irritated or anxious and toward the more helpful feeling of conscious gratitude.

"A grateful heart is a magnet for miracles."

Anonymous

in the tub or shower

Whether you are in and out of the shower in five minutes or enjoy
luxuriating for longer, clearing your mind while you clean your body
is a great combination. Many people find they have their most
creative thoughts while relaxing in the tub, so it is a valuable time
for contemplating gratitude, too.

when waking up or before you go to sleep

There is a lot to be said for keeping a notebook by your bed. Many of
us have our clearest or most creative thoughts just before we go to
sleep or in half-slumber before waking. Gratitude for past kindnesses,
memories of loving support, or thoughts of a gesture we could
make to someone who is in need or has been generous: these things
may come to mind more readily when we are not focusing on them
directly. Make a note before the thoughts slip away.

CHAPTER 3

giving, receiving, and reciprocating

Gratitude is a dance of give and take (literally), and the gift lies as much in the joy of giving as in the pleasure of receiving—and sometimes more so. For acceptance is in itself a gift, and a precious one at that.

Giving, receiving, and reciprocating lie at the heart of families, communities, and the civilized world as we know it. When we share, we all thrive and survive—and we develop a sense of care and belonging. Receiving a gift that has meaning tells us that we have been recognized and accepted for who we are. A thank you offered with heart is also a gift of love and appreciation. When we give rather than take, the whole world feels like a better and more generous place to be.

giving

Gratitude is associated with giving and with whole-hearted appreciation in all its various forms. When we think about gratitude, we relate it to a wish to appreciate and celebrate, but at its core, giving is about sharing and reaching out to others. The word comes from the Latin word *gratia*, meaning grace, graciousness, or gratefulness. It is not only a feeling—it can also become a state of being.

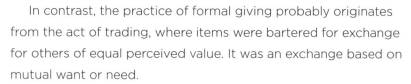

In contrast, the practice of formal giving probably originates from the act of trading, where items were bartered for exchange for others of equal perceived value. It was an exchange based on mutual want or need.

The distinction between "gratitude" and "gift" is subtle, but important: material gifts are symbolic exchanges, whereas gratitude comes from or through ourselves. It is linked to feelings of acceptance—which is perhaps why a generous but perfunctory gift given without heart can feel soulless, whereas the simplest gesture given with heart can feel like the most precious item in the world.

The word is also associated with the gift of our innate talents. In the early centuries, the "gifts" of prophecy, speaking in tongues, and healing were considered to come through, rather than from, the giver. We still refer to talents and skills—such as the ability to sing, play music, think mathematically, dance, play sport, or paint—as our

"People may forget what you said or forget what you did, but they will never forget how you made them feel."

Anonymous

natural gifts. These days, the gift of love plays an important role in spiritual traditions around the world, as well as in our lives in general. Personal gifts have come to symbolize feelings, so a very basic item can become imbued with meaning if it has been chosen with love and care. A rock collected on a clifftop walk may summon up memories of a special day; a single rose may be given in full awareness of all that it symbolizes; and a graduation gift may increase in emotional value as the years go by, as it represents a rite of passage and the love and respect of others.

paying attention—the dilemma of choosing a gift

A beautiful parcel can be a joy to behold and the unwrapping a moment to be treasured. When choosing a gift, the more important the person is to you, the greater your wish will be to come up with something ideal, meaningful, memorable, and possibly original, too. So deciding to give someone a gift is about much more than choosing a present. When we put time aside to focus on someone who holds meaning for us, we begin to reflect on ourselves, too:

- *Would she like this?*

- *Does he have one?*

- *If I get it wrong, will he/she think I don't care?*

- *Will he want one?*

- *Why don't I know more about his/her taste?*

- *Will it suit her?*

Remember: Give gifts thoughtfully

As adults, we find it easier to give than to receive, so it is important to respect one another's needs, and to consider our wish to give from the receiver's perspective as well as our own. Good intentions swiftly turn to panic when too much is riding on getting it "right." Each time we doubt ourselves, we are really asking: Why haven't I paid greater attention?

Whatever the style of giving and whatever the occasion, it will always be the "right" gift when we give with good heart and have devoted some thought to our decision. If in doubt, ask! Not every gift has to be a surprise.

What kind of gift-giver are you?

- Do you spend hours choosing the "right" gift for every person and occasion?

- Do you spend time wrapping the gift beautifully, especially when you feel the contents are modest?

- Do you give money instead of a gift for fear of "getting it wrong?"

You may decide that giving a gift serves no purpose, and that a kindly written card or a meaningful call has more value.

It sometimes feels as if there are a lot of rules and rituals surrounding the act of giving. Some are fun, and become part of an occasion, but others may be embedded in a bygone time that has very little relevance today. More often than not, the gift of celebration is a gift in itself—it is the presence of friends and loved ones rather than presents that most of us prefer.

Who is giving to whom?

Gift-giving has a way of becoming stressful when it becomes more about personal need than the wish to honor someone else. Perhaps...

• The giver becomes so concerned about causing disappointment that they can no longer trust his or her own judgment to choose;

• In an effort to please, and in fear of being judged, the giver spends more money than he or she can afford;

• The receiver is more focused on his or her own needs and wants than on the care the giver has taken.

The greatest gifts are not material gifts at all. They are expressed through the real time we choose to spend with one another, the genuine acknowledgment that we offer for things that are done for us, and our voiced recognition of the time, effort, and care involved in those loving gifts. There is a time-honored rhythm to gratitude. It is a three-step waltz of giving, receiving, and reciprocating.

keeping things special

Children, especially, look forward each year to birthday celebrations, festivities, and times of giving with enormous hope and excitement. Seeing a child's face as they receive and unwrap a gift is a precious treat in itself. No wonder so many parents and grandparents buy more and more lavish gifts to enjoy the reward of an excited child's grateful smile.

But gifts lose their glister when we receive them too often. Expectations become greater and the magic of receiving diminishes, because it is no longer rare or special. It's the gift equivalent of your favorite song being played endlessly on the radio, or the festive lights losing their magic if they stay up after the party is over.

When anticipation is high and imagination vivid, a promising parcel can produce great expectations, and disappointment can follow hard on the heels of hopes that are too high. So we learn early on that gifts are not necessarily all they seem: the simplest gift can be the most exciting, and the plainest parcel may contain the most surprising and wonderful reward.

In time, and with guidance, children learn not to expect, but to be open to receiving and always to appreciate, in which case they may be pleasantly surprised and rarely disappointed.

respectful giving

Have you ever had the experience of offering help to someone, only to have your offer refused? Those who are parents know only too well how that can feel. We all like to be appreciated, so when an offer of help is thrown back at us, it can feel like personal rejection. Before taking it personally, however, it can help to pause and think again— about how it may seem from the other person's point of view.

If life feels tough and you have been struggling in some way, the chances are that your sense of self has taken a battering, too. So when someone insists on giving you something that you do not feel you need, or that will make no tangible difference to the reality of your situation, it simply reinforces the lack that you already feel. A person with a disability, who has learned to live independently, may rebuff a well-meaning arm to help them get on a train because they have had to cope unassisted for years; an elderly person who is feeling lonely may turn down a one-off invitation to lunch because coming home to an empty house reinforces the sense of aloneness; a homeless man who would love to eat turns down a tuna sandwich because, although he is hungry, he does not like tuna—and although he is in need, he is still able to exercise his right to choose.

Respect for others must be at the heart of any act of giving—and that means asking the person what kind of help they would like (if any). Giving without asking is not giving at all, it is about satisfying our own need to feel good about ourselves.

Remember: Time is the greatest gift you can give

gratitude in action

Giving a gift is a special way to show gratitude, and need not be expensive. Choosing something with wit, care, originality, or attention to detail has far more value than a luxury label.

simple ways to create a personal gift

• Take a special photograph, and get family, friends, or colleagues to sign the mount. It will immediately become precious, even before you put it in a frame. (This idea came from my cousin Nicole, who corralled our entire family for this purpose before a very special wedding.)

• Buy real ribbon made of natural fiber to tie up your parcels. It often costs no more than synthetic ribbon, and it makes your gift look extra-special. If possible, deliver the packages in person.

• Pass on a favorite book, DVD, or CD. It will mean even more to the recipient to know that it was yours and that you loved it. To make the gift extra-special, include some treats that your friend or relative can enjoy while watching or listening (a pair of snuggle socks or a big candy bar, perhaps). This is not my idea. I was once lucky enough to receive just such a package—and it was a very precious gift indeed.

• Bake! Homemade cookies or cake are always welcome, even if you are not a confident baker.

• Create a simple posy of handpicked flowers, grasses, or leaves, containing an odd number of each element, such as three or five.

• Give something away. Most of us own far more than we need. As adults we may be hanging on to items that were precious to us in younger years—clothes or toys or paraphernalia from long-lost hobbies—but that someone else could be gaining pleasure from now. Giving things away is enormously liberating, especially when you know that objects from your past are adding joy to someone's present.

gratitude guru: **Martin Seligman**

"I don't think you can have a positive future unless you can envision one."

Martin Seligman (1942–)

The internationally renowned psychologist Professor Martin Seligman is director of the Penn Positive Psychology Center at Pennsylvania State University. Commonly referred to as the founder of the concept of positive psychology, he has spent his career researching the factors that contribute to pessimism or optimism in outlook, and whether these characteristics are innate or learned. The findings are endlessly fascinating. An inspirational academic with the ability to communicate his ideas more broadly, his books include *Flourish* (2011), *Authentic Happiness* (2002), and *Learned Optimism* (1990). All are international bestsellers.

Professor Seligman has devised a series of measures that help to prove that those with a "can do" attitude, who believe that they have control over their life, and who understand that they can choose how to respond to adversity or obstacles, tend to be in better physical health and more resilient. They may even live longer. Pessimists, on the other hand, who don't believe that anything they do will change their circumstances, are triggering activity in the brain that encourages "learned helplessness." The findings tend to show that they are less resistant when illness strikes, and may even die younger than those who show optimism.

Optimistic people are not necessarily more grateful than pessimists. However, research is showing that practicing gratitude may be the key to enabling pessimists to become more optimistic.

receiving

"We cannot hold a torch to light another person's path without shining light to guide our own way too."

Anonymous

When someone gives a gift or gives of themselves, someone else receives and accepts what that person wished to share. Giving and receiving are the yin and yang of the exchange. Neither can exist without the other. It is a balanced ritual that extends back beyond the dawn of the world's religions.

There are few things in life that can lift our spirits more than hearing from someone we care about. Receiving letters, telephone calls, gifts, kind words, or symbols of love and recognition help to cement our feeling of belonging and being cared for. Receiving is also about gaining wisdom; about tuning in to the world around us and its impact on our senses; about noticing beauty in all its forms; and about appreciating the existence of other creatures who share this planet. Occasionally it involves feeling emotionally vulnerable. Receiving is not always straightforward.

Most of all, receiving is about acceptance. When someone offers you a present, they are truly offering you their presence, too. The gift becomes a symbol of your friendship, acquaintance, or other relationship. They have given you not only a gift, but also their time, attention, and care. Take time to savor it. Adjust your human antennae for a moment and tune in to the person who is paying you this compliment. What does their gesture tell you about them? How does their kindness reflect on you? Have you the generosity of spirit to let someone truly enjoy the moment of giving?

gratitude in action

Show gratitude for what you've received by collecting memories.

the perpetual gratitude jar

Create a personal pot of gratitude with ideas for ways to say thank you. This can be a real jar or a metaphorical jar, depending on whether you want a physical reminder or whether the act of contemplating the jar is enough to focus your thoughts. The gratitude jar is a place where you can keep the names of the people you feel grateful toward and want to spend time with or write to or thank, as well as ideas and suggestions for expressions of thankfulness. The beauty of the gratitude jar is that the positivity is automatically generated as you remove ideas randomly to take action, and put new ones back in, in place of the old, for use in the future.

1. Random gratitude method:

Add names of those you wish to thank on pieces of paper of one color, and ways to say thank you on pieces of paper of another color. Choose two pieces of paper, one of each color, to marry up ideas for giving. This approach needs to be treated as a starting point for ideas and as a bit of fun. Choosing "Great Aunt Millie" and "Sky-dive treat" may not be the ideal combination!

2. Focused gratitude method:

The pot is the ideal place to turn all your guilty "shoulds" into positive action—write down specific ideas and choose one at random every so often. For example:

Take Lily to the mall this weekend.

Treat Mom to a girls' lunch.

Bake Tom a birthday cake this year.

Phone Maud to find out about her health.

Book a weekend to see Grandma.

Put together a surprise care package for Mike.

the great wall of gratitude

This could be a pinboard, the fridge, or an area of your home where you keep photographs, sketches, or other objects to remind you of key people in your life, for whom you have heartfelt appreciation. Most people build these up over time, and it is often an organic process, as postcards and photos arrive from various corners of the world. In our increasingly digital world, however, printed reminders are fewer and farther between. It is important to keep a store of visual images to embed key memories and remind you of the important people and events in your life.

GRATITUDE IN PRACTICE:

Seeing the positive

Marion recalls a time when she was given a spinning wheel as a gift from an elderly friend who could no longer spin. "I was so delighted with the gift," she says, "that I over-did the spinning and developed an injury that prevented me from pursuing my other love: music. It took time, but I was eventually able to feel gratitude for the downtime as it allowed me to read more and to pay attention by listening to music, and also to start learning a new language—none of which I had time for previously."

reciprocating

"It is not happiness that makes us grateful;
it is gratefulness that makes us happy."

David Steindl-Rast (1926–)

Reciprocation is all about maintaining a balance. If we receive without giving, we may feel lesser versions of ourselves; if our generosity is refused, we may feel rejected. For the dance to work in harmony we must be willing to receive as well as to give, to accept thanks as well as offer praise, and to be ready to offer our support to those who need help, simply because we are in a position where we can.

This section also dips in to the tricky area of feeling beholden, or the feelings of anger or resentment that may arise when receiving a gift or generous gesture suggests that the gift is being given for a less than straightforward reason, and that therefore something about the exchange is out of balance.

Thankfulness is not always an easy or a natural emotion. It can be difficult to feel grateful when facing intense hardship. Sometimes previous experiences trigger emotions that block the capacity for giving or receiving, and there seems to be little reason to feel appreciation. Reciprocation is not always direct. A kindness given to one person may be "passed on" via a kind act to another instead.

the joy of thanks

The foundations of gratitude begin in childhood. Young children's thank-you letters are often a joy—free-flowing and half-formed, short on spelling, with a few crayon scribbles for illustrative effect, they are often tucked away lovingly and kept for years by the recipient. When children say thank you, they pause to appreciate what has been given to them and remember in a more conscious way the fact that they have been valued.

Of course, few children actually enjoy writing thank-you letters, and that makes it hard for parents when they try to insist that they should. But for the giver who has put heart and time into choosing and wrapping the gift, a silence shouts not only a lack of thankfulness, but also a lack of care. The strength of feeling that the giver poured into giving the gift is reabsorbed as a negative reward. Even those who swear that they were not expecting a thank you will be affected in this way.

Saying thank you is good for us. It helps to "seal the deal," as those early traders understood.

when you have nothing at all to give, give anyway

Imagine that you are on your way to buy groceries. A middle-aged man is near the entrance of the store, playing a few notes—badly—on a penny whistle, his cap on the ground to invite donations. He is dressed scruffily and appears not to have bathed in a while.

Some people do not notice; some do not wish to see. Others see but are filled with fear and so do not approach him, although he is not dangerous. Occasionally someone pauses to offer him a few coins for his cap.

Each time someone speaks to him or gives him something, the man thanks them, sincerely and profusely—which means they walk away feeling good about themselves, even though he still does not have anywhere near enough money for an evening meal or a bed for

"In the best, the friendliest and simplest relations, flattery or praise is necessary, just as grease is necessary to keep wheels turning."

Leo Tolstoy (1828–1910), *War and Peace*

the night, or even a drink, if that is his choice. When you watch more closely you notice that it is not the people with shopping carts piled high with purchases who are giving to the man, it is those who are moved by compassion and appear not to have much themselves, or an older person who seems alone, or a young person who has not yet learned to judge someone for their weaknesses.

Often in life it is the person with the least who ends up giving the most. When we give to others, we feel better about ourselves, and when we reciprocate the giving makes us feel emotionally in balance. There is giving and there is receiving, but it is in reciprocation that the magic happens. That is where human connection lies, and where there is equality in all things.

Did you know?

The University of California, Berkeley, runs the grateful-sounding Greater Good Science Center, which funds research into the long-term benefits of gratitude. Scientists at the center have discovered that people who practice gratitude regularly have been found to:

• Develop stronger immune systems and lower blood pressure

• Experience higher levels of positive emotion

• Have an increased sense of joy, optimism, and happiness

• Be more likely to act with generosity and compassion

• Feel less lonely and isolated

Visit their website to find out more about the latest research in this area (see Further Resources, page 141).

GRATITUDE IN PRACTICE:

Stepping into gratitude

Maria was in her forties when, through a series of unexpected circumstances, she took in a homeless young woman, who was pregnant. Maria had very little in the way of financial resources, but she hadn't stopped to think twice about offering the young woman a home. After taking advice she was told that some financial support was likely to be available. The advice turned out to be misguided, however, and no external funds were available. Determined to act with love and compassion, Maria decided to look her lack of funds in the face and turn it into a gift. Each week she handed the young woman an allowance and told her that it was her contribution to their mutual household budget. She was to choose for herself the food she would like to eat, and prepare several meals for them both each week. The transformation was remarkable. The young woman not only treated the allowance with respect and bought food carefully, but also discovered a talent for creative cooking that she didn't know she had. When the baby arrived she had the confidence to know that she could prepare meals and manage a budget. Maria's loving kindness was met with the kind of gratitude that makes a friend for life.

gratitude in action

Practicing gratitude is about giving back, appreciating consciously, and creating a balance. The following suggestions will lead you to think of your own, too:

one person whom I have never thanked properly

As we saw on pages 29–30, writing a letter of heartfelt gratitude to someone who you feel has made a significant difference to your life can have an incredibly powerful and positive effect on both the writer and the reader.

Take some time to think of someone who has had an impact on your health or well-being, or on the direction your life has taken. Then, seize the moment and call them—or, at the very least, mail a letter. The benefit to your well-being will be immense.

The gift of belonging

A team at the University of Southern California is looking into the benefits gratitude has on health and well-being. They are discovering that our simple habit of saying "thank you" goes far beyond being a ritual social exchange. Gratitude in all forms makes us feel appreciated, which stimulates areas of the brain that are linked to empathy, moral judgment, and bonding. Dr. Glenn Fox, who is leading the study, says he designed the experiment to assess the commonalities between "small feelings of appreciation and large feelings of gratitude." His team is discovering that patterns of brain activity show gratitude to be "a complex social emotion that is really built around how others seek to benefit us." It plays an important role in our sense of who we are as human beings, how we relate to and care for one another, and our sense of social belonging.

the gratitude tree

Trees of all shapes and species are a wonderful symbol of the way that gratitude grows and envelops and nourishes us, providing the oxygen we need to thrive and survive.

The gratitude tree is sown from seeds of kindness and spreads via the roots of belonging. Gratitude grows like the solid trunk of an ancient oak, generating connectedness through its branches via the acts of giving, receiving, and reciprocating. As it matures over the seasons, the beautiful foliage of acceptance emerges, creating a canopy of ever-varying color and offering protection to all, and of course it bears the fruit of love, friendship, happiness, and forgiveness—that germinate further acts of kindness and spread the roots of gratitude further.

For the gratitude tree to thrive, there is an additional nutrient required in the earth that feeds the roots—and that is trust. Trust that the gifts are bestowed with no artificial additive of expectation; and that the tree will be nurtured with goodwill and watered with appreciation—to protect it from neglect or drought.

Ebb and flow

Sometimes a gift is so generous that accepting it can be difficult—house repairs, a loan for a car, college fees, babysitting, lifts to hospital. Barriers get in the way of acceptance, such as fear of feeling beholden, a sense of unworthiness, worries about not being able to reciprocate, or loss of self-respect. However, my father has a lovely philosophy about giving and receiving, which he refers to as "ebb and flow." All it means is that energy, time, money, and companionship are all resources that are needed at different ages and stages of life, and all can be exchanged as time goes by.

making time for gratitude

A sense of gratitude can be developed consciously, either as a coping strategy when life does not turn out quite as planned, or simply as a way of appreciating the "here and now."

giving thanks for skills and abilities

Gratitude is not always about other people. Have you stopped lately to think about your own unique talents and abilities? Even if you lack confidence, you will know where your strengths and weaknesses lie— what you do well and can enhance, and what you need to work on and can improve.

Feeling stuck? Unsure what your skills might be? Try asking those around you what they feel you do well. It can be as simple as being able to make the perfect cup of coffee, making sure that people feel cared for by always remembering birthdays, or offering newcomers a warm welcome.

List three skills and abilities that you feel grateful for. You may like to include:

1. A note of why you appreciate these talents.

2. An observation or compliment made by someone else that you can accept wholeheartedly.

3. A deeper thought about your vision for your skills and talents in the future.

1.
_____
_____

2.
_____
_____

3.
_____
_____

If negative thoughts strike and threaten to crush the positive ones, pause to acknowledge your feelings and try to understand why they have cropped up to sabotage you at this time. Are you able to introduce a positive thought to counterbalance the negative? Ask yourself how and whether you can change the status quo.

stop to appreciate the "unsung heroes" in your daily life

Who are the people whose work you benefit from each day, who are rarely acknowledged for their dedication? For example:

• The cleaner who focuses on the craftsmanship that went into making the sweep of the staircase that she dusts every day, instead of seeing her repetitive work as a chore.

• The nurse who has a waiting room full of patients, but still manages to greet every single person by name and with a smile, instead of focusing on the number of blood samples she has taken that day.

• The receptionist at the motel who speaks directly to your elderly mother and connects with her sense of humor, rather than judging her for her age and her wheelchair.

Thinking about the people who touch your life indirectly helps to bring them into your consciousness when you are going about your daily tasks, so you are more likely to show appreciation or praise, and acknowledge them or mention them to other people. That is how gratitude grows and spreads.

CHAPTER 4

acceptance

(or when gratitude is difficult)

Sometimes in life we are pitched a curveball. It can be hard to feel any sense of gratitude in the midst of a tragedy, illness, or disaster. But it is when we have the most to lose that we also have the most to gain. When life as we know it is torn away, we are left with a greater awareness of what is most important.

This section takes a good look at how to cope when gratitude is difficult, and offers ways to reframe life's challenges with hope and forgiveness—and generosity.

why me, why this, why now?

Gratitude does not come readily or immediately in every situation. It is highly unlikely, when a crisis strikes, that your first feelings will be of gratitude for the pain and suffering you are facing. A fractured leg? Thank you for the downtime! A broken heart? Great—I knew it was about time I experienced a period of loss and abandonment! Out of work? Bring it on—I am so pleased that I can no longer afford the payments on my house. A serious illness? Let's not even go there … no one would ever want to put their family or themselves through the trauma and fear of a life-threatening diagnosis.

And yet, and yet … many, many people (although by no means all), after coming through a period of difficulty, will look back on their experience as a gift of some sort. The enforced period of recovery from accident or illness allowed time for reflection, or brought their family closer together; an unwanted redundancy led to a change of professional direction or a slimming-down of stressful financial commitments; a broken relationship is seen in hindsight from a healthier perspective—and the future represents something more positive. But while we are in the midst of disruption, gratitude can be elusive.

feeling lost

If you are in the middle of a dark forest and no one knows you are there, it is clear that there is little point in waiting to be found. You have to accept that you are lost. You may try to find your own way out, making determined efforts to keep warm, build a shelter, and avoid predators—but without experience, support, or knowledge of your terrain you may simply put yourself in greater danger.

> "*Life isn't all ha ha hee hee.*"

Meera Syal CBE (1961–), writer and actor

Eventually, in order to get help, you create a din, clear a space, light a fire—do whatever is necessary to get yourself noticed, ideally without doing permanent damage or putting yourself in greater danger. In life, as in the forest, those who are in crisis may create a situation that requires the support of others—with luck, before it is too late for them to be saved.

To step toward gratitude we may first need to find the courage to face the reality of the present moment and ask for help. It is not only the person who feels lost who needs acceptance, but also those who offer love, support, or solace.

grateful acceptance

How, then, can we learn to cope with our feelings when we are in the midst of trauma and distress? How can we find the will to play the long game and to look beyond the pain and discomfort of the present moment? The truth is that there is no easy answer. For some there will be the pathway to meditation or prayer, for others the comfort of friends and family—or the kindness of strangers. What is common to both routes, however, is taking a conscious decision to step away from our feelings of fear and isolation, or let go of the sense that we are alone with our fears and troubles, and try to look outward, to start reconnecting with the world around us.

In the words of the gratitude expert Robert Emmons, "Life is suffering. No amount of positive thinking exercises will change this truth." He acknowledges clearly through his research that forcibly adopting an artificially positive stance during times of trauma can have the opposite effect. "Keep calm and carry on" might be the only mantra you can manage at times of pressure.

transformation

Grateful acceptance is the state of fully absorbing the present state of affairs and seeking to discover what can be learned from it, what our role is within it, and how we can eventually feel grateful for the experience. There is no substitute for time and patience. It is through the cracks of life's darker and more challenging moments that we can see where the light shines most brightly.

We may be surprised to find that, following a period of distress and disturbance, our capacity for happiness and contentment gradually starts to increase. We start to focus on the good instead of the bad. We rediscover the joy in small things. Material things diminish in importance and we focus instead on the quality of our relationships. Most of all, we feel a sense of gratitude—for this, for here, for now.

GRATITUDE IN PRACTICE:

Keeping faith

On August 5, 2010, in Atacama, Chile, 33 miners were trapped underground when part of a mine collapsed, leaving all exit routes blocked. Dismay turned to hope when the rescue team found a note that told anxious families that the miners were alive. Sixty-nine days later, following a remarkable feat of skilled engineering, all the miners were rescued to a sense of overwhelming gratitude that was felt the world over.

thought swapping

One way of coming to terms with living through a difficult time is to find a way of getting a new perspective on the experience. Reframing our thoughts is a subtle but powerful way of putting ourselves back into the driving seat of our own lives. For example:

Remember: Reframe your thoughts

• If you find yourself thinking, *"I am so fed up that X happened,"* try swapping it with, *"At least I can be glad that Y didn't happen."*

• *"I am so fed up with having to chase my kids to get out of bed every morning,"* could become, *"I am so glad that my kids are still young enough to need me—but it is time they learned to take personal responsibility for getting themselves up in the morning."*

• *"I wish people didn't come to me to offload all their problems,"* might become, *"I hope I helped in some way, and it is good to know that I am trusted."*

• Feeling that *"I am so tired of having to go to the doctor for tests"* is completely understandable, but it becomes easier to handle if it is reframed as, *"I am glad to have these tests underway and am grateful that the doctor is taking them seriously."*

"*Opportunity is the gift within every gift.*"

David Steindl-Rast (1926–)

gratitude guru: **Robert A. Emmons**

"When we are grateful we affirm that a source of goodness exists in our lives."

Robert A. Emmons (1958–)

Professor Robert A. Emmons is considered to be the world's leading scientific expert on the study of gratitude. He is a professor of psychology at the University of California in Davis.

Professor Emmons' books and work are vitally important because he is providing and building scientific evidence that demonstrates that ideas based on gratitude lead to greater happiness and a better quality of life. The research conducted by his school of psychology is proving gradually that increased gratitude can lead to greater emotional well-being, better relationships, and greater resilience, and is also associated with a better quality of life. He considers gratitude to be an act of celebration, and describes it as a heightened and focused intellectual and emotional state of appreciation. His work embraces the spiritual element of gratitude, too, and he continues to investigate why gratitude makes such a positive impact on our life.

letting go

Anyone who has faced a painful loss of any kind will know the mixed emotions that can arise, and how hard it can be to step forward into a new phase of life. Sometimes we get stuck in a cycle of looking backward, with regret, guilt, anger, or sadness. In the words of the British novelist L.P. Hartley, "The past is a foreign country: they do things differently there." Focusing on might-have-beens has the potential to cut us off from future possibilities. In the short term, the gracious way to reframe your thought processes is by seeking positivity amid the difficulty.

• *"I am grateful to have discovered that I am stronger and more resilient than I realized."*

• *"I'm so glad for what we had. We had a lot of fun together and I am grateful for those happy times."*

• *"I appreciate the way my partner put the children's needs before his own when we divorced."*

• *"I will be eternally grateful for the gracious kindness and attention that we received from the hospital's care team."*

GRATITUDE IN PRACTICE:

Experiencing freedom

Robin, 44, is a recovering cancer patient. "Extreme suffering becomes in the end a form of liberation. When you have nothing left to lose you no longer care what anyone thinks. When you no longer fear death, you are free to live the better life that you always wanted." He and his family have found a new sense of gratitude in the simple joy of being in each other's company. "The little things no longer irritate," says Robin's wife. "Every day feels more precious now."

don't go it alone

This chapter was very nearly called "Hope," because embedded in that word is a sense of trust and positivity. When we carry hope in our hearts we believe that things can change for the better—against all odds. Asking for help may be part of that process, and a very healthy part at that. When hope works hand-in-hand with help, our personal dreams of a better future are more likely to become a reality. Asking for help also allows us to step toward a life where gratitude plays a stronger role.

crossing the bridge

Many of us have been brought up to be stoical in the face of problems or adversity. Brits, especially, are known for their "stiff upper lip" under pressure (that is, not showing emotion).

The trouble with adopting this approach is that emotions are suppressed. We can't switch off our feelings, but when we bury or deny them they have a way of coming back to bite us in other forms: as inappropriate anger, coldness, over-sensitivity to stress, insomnia, the inability to express emotion, addictive behavior, and so on.

Independence builds walls, not bridges. If you find yourself habitually consumed by disappointment, with few expectations of hope or happiness, don't suffer in silence. Talk to friends to get a new perspective, or have a chat with your doctor. There may be other ways to help you get through this temporary tough time.

Working together or discussing problems provides a broader perspective. Collaboration and conversation are the bridges that generate new perspective and understanding that is greater than anything we could imagine alone, and in doing so we put competition and ego aside. We feel grateful for the outcome. Gratitude is a leveler. It reminds us that we are all connected and part of something greater than ourselves.

A Franciscan blessing

(Thirteenth century)

May you be blessed with discomfort at easy answers, half-truths, and superficial relationships—so that you may live deep within your heart.

May you be blessed with anger at injustice, oppression, and exploitation of people—so that you may work for justice, freedom, and peace.

May you be blessed with tears shed for those who suffer pain, rejection, hunger, and war—so that you may reach out your hand to comfort them and turn their pain to joy.

May you be blessed with enough foolishness to believe that you can make a difference to the world—so that you can do what others claim cannot be done, to bring justice and kindness to our children and to the poor.

combating cynicism

Sourness and cynicism have a way of crushing feel-good moments. Careworn thoughts of "What does he/she really want?" can take the edge off the pleasure of receiving an unplanned visit or enjoying a spontaneous gift.

Receiving with negativity in our hearts means that we suffer pain from something that may have been given with genuine kindness. Not speaking up to say how we feel means that the person doesn't have the chance to realize the impact of their actions.

In her book *The Business Alchemist*, the leadership coach Pilar Godino talks about each of us being motivated either to move toward or away from something in our conversation. Toward sentences are full of positivity and connection; away from sentences are negative and pull away from the risk of being hurt. For example:

• *"My son only ever calls me when he wants something"* is an away from sentence. The corresponding toward statement is *"I have a good relationship with my son and I love it when he calls. He knows that I will say no if I cannot help for some reason."*

• *"My sister only gave me the furniture because she no longer has space for it"* (away from), instead of, *"She is a star for giving me first refusal"* (toward).

• *"If I hadn't called my friend she would not have invited me"* (away from), instead of, *"The party should be fun. I need to keep in touch better"* (toward).

• *"My boyfriend gave me flowers. He must be feeling guilty"* (away from), instead of, *"The flowers are lovely, but it's out of character for him to splash out. I will have to ask him what is going on"* (toward).

Becoming aware of how we use language when we talk to ourselves can be a surprisingly strong way to bring more gratitude into our lives and relationships.

I wish, I want ...

You may like to take a moment to think of something you want or that you wish you had. Do these desires feel like a goal that you can achieve, or an entitlement that you lack? Notice how this makes you feel, and even how your posture responds or your facial expression changes as you contemplate your wishes.

When we focus only on the wanting, we remain powerless. If you think of your wishes as an entitlement, you may feel demotivated and resentful that they have not been fulfilled. If you think of them as goals, on the other hand, you will already be considering what actions you need to take to get you to where you want to be.

When we set ourselves goals, we become mentally grateful for our skills, knowledge, and experience. As we go forward we appreciate each step that we achieve because we are getting nearer to our goal—and we give thanks for getting that far.

In reality, our achievements do not come from outside of us, and they are rarely bestowed upon us. Instead, we must strive inwardly and work toward them, every step of the way. Feeling grateful for what we have and appreciative of the progress we are making is an ongoing state of being that keeps us on track.

gratitude in action

Capturing the story of your family in a visual or recorded form can help to provide strength in difficult times because it brings everyone together, reminding them of precious moments and their place in the story. It allows a way for everyone to share their thoughts and feelings, leading to reconciliation and renewed understanding. The outcome may provide an heirloom for future generations, too.

one stitch at a time

In the United States and Canada there is a very strong tradition of quilting that dates back to the pioneering days of the nineteenth century. With no modern technology or television to while away the evenings, the women of the time would sew, create, and embroider their family stories and memories, with enormous care and skill, into the very fabric of the quilt. Memory quilts were created in gratitude and remembrance for those who were lost to illness, war, or old age. They were also a tribute to a life that had been left behind. The quilts were lovingly sewn in memory, or for a special occasion. Fragments of clothing were sometimes used in the quilts, and many of the finished items were embroidered with a signature. Nearly 200 years later, these unique records of family history have become treasured heirlooms that are passed down from one generation to the next. Births, weddings, deaths, birthdays, and anniversaries all offer good reasons for making a memory quilt, and an excuse to share family stories once again. It is a wonderful tradition that reinforces the personal memory of each family's unique heritage and history.

If you would like to try quilting and need ideas on how to start, try some of the web resources listed on page 141.

picture this

A current and rather more instant version of a
family quilt is the creation of a digital photo album
or Facebook page. Creating a place where
everyone in the family can post their memories
and share their stories can be a tremendous
source of enjoyment that is appreciated by everyone
and has the potential to be kept and shared forever. Memory
books and photo collages are a wonderful way to capture history
in the making.

Everyone of every age has their own memory of growing up
within your family. It can be fun to ask everyone to contribute their
thoughts—and to write down a favorite story, a reason for gratitude,
or what they like best about being in your family.

telling your story

Getting together to share memories and stories, rather like creating
a quilt, can keep memories alive and bring about a new sense of
gratitude and connectedness. Whether it is getting together with a
group of friends or a special occasion when the whole family meets,
encouraging everyone to come with a personal story or something
else to share can generate a lively and memorable occasion with
special permanent mementoes of the day and of a particular moment
in time.

mementoes from the past

Every family heirloom tells a story, but the detail can get lost over
time. Are there items of jewelry, medals, ornaments, pictures, or
furniture that have special meaning? Who in your family knows the
background? Keeping a note of who gave what to whom, when, and
in what context will be endlessly interesting to future generations.
They will be grateful for the care you have taken, as your notes will
bring the past back to life.

making time for gratitude

Being "glad" may not be a panacea for future happiness, and "thinking positive" doesn't guarantee that everything will turn out all right, but it does seems that conscious gratitude is connected to optimism and forgiveness, which are likely to lead to positive action and eventual change.

taking stock

Try taking a moment to complete the following sentences:

I am grateful that _____

happened because _____

_____

I am grateful to _____

because _____

_____

I am grateful for this moment because _____

_____

Gratitude is not necessarily an immediate response. Sometimes the statements need to be repeated, to enable you to drill deeper, and to still the quiet voice of resistance. Over time, and with practice, when feelings of anger or impatience surface, having a few gratitude anchors in your mental armory can help to diffuse an uncomfortable or upsetting situation.

choosing change

Think about how you can actively work toward change by trying to complete the lists below.

Three things I feel dissatisfied with that I can change positively:

1.
_____
_____

2.
_____
_____

3.
_____
_____

Two people who could help me to look at my situation in another way:

1.
_____
_____

2.
_____
_____

One thing I can start to change from today:

1.
_____
_____

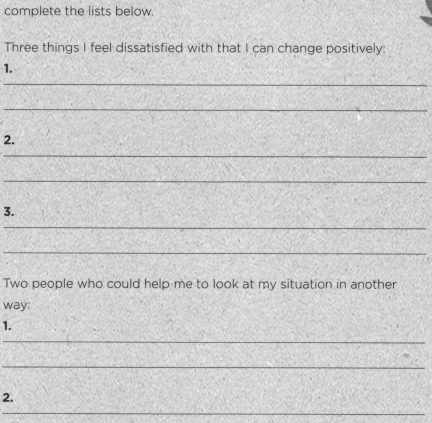

showing appreciation

True gratitude has a way of generating a warm sense of appreciation. But what does this really mean?

The literal meaning of appreciation is to price something. When we say thank you in appreciation, we are saying clearly, "I put a great value on what you have done," and when we are moved to take action because we appreciate what someone is going through, we are expressing an understanding of the true cost of their experiences—in every sense of the word. An action that is offered in gratitude and received with appreciation seals the deal. It becomes an equal exchange.

taking action

Far from being a passive response, showing appreciation resonates deep within us and propels us into action. It leads us to find ways to give back and make a constructive difference—whether expressing a simple thank you, doing a return favor, running a half-marathon to raise funds, or taking steps to safeguard and protect the people, places, or creatures for which we are grateful.

It would be hard to feel conscious appreciation and gratitude while simultaneously being unkind or bad-tempered. The practice of daily gratitude therefore shores us up against rash actions that we might otherwise regret. Feeling appreciative has the capacity to make the world a better place.

This is all very easy to say, of course, but how does the theory work in practice? Gratitude is a habit that we must cultivate constantly if we are to gain the benefits. Developing the gratitude habit starts by paying attention to the people who are in our life every day, and offering them expressions of appreciation and kindness. It moves on to appreciating ourselves and the role we play in our own relationships, as well as the world at large and all the creatures and beauty within it. It begins, however, with small steps, and with focusing on the everyday.

"As we express our gratitude, we must never forget that the highest appreciation is not to utter words, but to live by them."

John F. Kennedy (1917–1963), politician and 35th President of the United States

everyday appreciation

"Have I told you lately (that I love you)?"

Van Morrison, 1989

There is no greater gift than to be loved and accepted, and to know that we are appreciated for who we are and for the things we do. Our feelings for the people we value most in life become a powerful force that gives us a sense of connectedness.

Feeling gratitude and showing appreciation are subtly different. Gratitude is a wholehearted emotion that tends to hit us full-on, instinctively, when something positive happens to us. Appreciation, on the other hand, turns goodwill and positive intentions into a conscious act of thanks and thankfulness. Appreciation is also a sign of respect, so its impact can be swept away very easily if there is any sign of it being expressed begrudgingly or without sincerity.

Showing appreciation is an act of acceptance. It takes us outside of ourselves and turns the focus on to others: the people, places, creatures, or events that have made a difference to our lives, through their kindness, support, love, or inspiration. However, sometimes we are so busy being busy that we forget to let people know quite how grateful we are to have them in our lives.

making time for family

Relationships within families can be complicated, and may change over time. Even when we are fortunate enough to have strong bonds with our siblings, cousins, or parents, the chances are that we take our loved ones for granted much of the time. One of the easiest ways of showing gratitude, especially to parents and grandparents, is simply to offer them the gift of your time. That means time with full attention intact, and possibly a strong dose of patience, too—with both ears in action (especially if you are talking by phone).

• Do you have a relative whom you have not seen for some time? Is it time to give him or her a call to show your appreciation?

• How much of your life do you share with your parents and grandparents? Do you involve them to some extent, or are you living in a parallel universe?

• How much do you know about their lives? For example, do you know what they studied at school or whether they enjoyed sport?

• How often do you ask them to tell you about their past? How did they meet? What is their story?

• When you think back over your life, what have you learned from your parents, and what childhood moments do you feel grateful for?

• If there were troubled times, are you able to find ways to understand with appreciation and forgiveness in your heart?

We are on this little planet for too short a spell not to make the most of the time we have together, even if the going gets tough and we fall out sometimes.

the joy of friends

Showing gratitude and appreciation for our closest friends tends to be one of the easiest things in the world. We know how they think, what they like, what makes them laugh—and what they would most appreciate. We tend to be more relaxed and able to be ourselves with our friends than with our family. Even so, it is possible to take someone we care about for granted, inadvertently.

• When you think of your friendship circle, do some people get the fun assignments while others get the angst?

• When you get in touch, do you respect their time? Or do you expect them to "drop everything" and be there for you?

The person whom you turn toward to talk through your woes is not always the same person you choose to go partying with, although you probably appreciate them equally. Showing conscious appreciation is an important part of building friendships and becomes increasingly important as we get older.

GRATITUDE IN PRACTICE:

Kindness and inspiration

Gratitude stems from kindness and inspiration that appear in unexpected places. At a time when the deadline for this book was getting ever nearer, I was due to stay with some great friends. I was looking forward to seeing them but extremely anxious about the impact on my work. It had been a challenging time—my ancient computer had decided to give up the ghost and I was behind schedule. Then my car broke down. There was no way I could go—although the "donkey" (see page 33) was that I could complete my book project. However, being the kind of people they are, they wouldn't take no for an answer, and insisted on driving 50 miles out of their way to come and pick me up.

En route to me, their vehicle broke down as well. Oh no! I received a disappointed text: "Sorry—but this one really is out of our hands." (I was secretly rather relieved!) Rather wonderfully, however, their insurance covered the provision of a hire car. They came to get me anyway.

After a lovely meal and great conversation, I pleaded work and headed for the guest room, at the top of the house. The walls were painted a deep blue, and covered in fluorescent stars that would begin glowing mysteriously when the lights went out. It had once been their daughter's room and was very peaceful. On the wall was a notice, which read: "Every day may not be good, but there is something good in every day." This is the perfect place for me to be, I thought—and sat down to write.

"I appreciate you when …"

Professor Sara Algoe has spent many years researching the role of gratitude in relationships. In a study of 47 couples between the ages of 24 and 40 (who had been together for an average of five years), she found a connection between being actively grateful and feeling more positive about each other. During the study, over the course of 30 consecutive days, some of the couples were asked to spend time together each day chatting about everyday things, while other couples were asked to spend time each day expressing gratitude to each other for the little things that had happened. The couples were also asked to complete a daily questionnaire, to find out how they were feeling about their relationship on a scale from 1 to 9. For example, in answer to the question "Today our relationship was …," the couples had to answer from 1 ("terrible") to 9 ("terrific").

Rather wonderfully, Professor Algoe discovered that in contrast to the couples who were just passing the time of day, the couples who were giving each other positive messages of gratitude found that their relationships had strengthened as a result. Receiving gratitude had made each person more likely to feel appreciated and therefore more motivated to express gratitude to the other person, too.

All too often in a long-term relationship, there is a gradual increase in finding fault and noticing what is lacking, rather than looking actively for what is good about each other.

When we *find* reasons to be grateful and feel positive about each other, and also *remind* each other that we appreciate each other, we start to appreciate ourselves more, too. Over time, this kind of positivity makes the individuals in a couple feel more confident about being "good at" relationships, and reinforces their feelings for each other. Although the research is not definitive, the results

The power of laughter

Gratitude often has a light, upbeat energy. Anyone who has ever heard the Dalai Lama speak or has seen a video of wise elders such as Nelson Mandela or Archbishop Desmond Tutu will know that even when they are talking about serious matters, they are never far from humor and sharing the sound of laughter. Sara Algoe has undertaken research in this area, too, and has found that laughter plays a crucial role in the way human beings relate to and appreciate one another. We feel closer to those who share our sense of humor. When we can share a belly laugh, we get on much better and work together more cooperatively. Could this finding provide a revolutionary approach to improving international relations and achieving world peace?

seem to show that a daily dose of appreciation and positivity *binds* us together more happily.

Of course, both people must be equally committed to expressing gratitude, and it also depends on how we express appreciation. Our tone of voice and the level of sincerity are all important. The memory expert Tony Buzan often remarks that we remember beginnings, endings, and points of difference more clearly than any other element within a conversation. So, no matter what you have discussed with your partner, if you start and end by expressing appreciation and gratitude, that is what he or she is most likely to remember.

"Find. Remind. Bind."

Professor Sara Algoe PhD, University of North Carolina

being alongside

Andrew is a well-loved chaplain at a school in England. In many ways he is the heart of the school, and the person to whom staff and students alike will turn in a crisis. He has wise guidance for those who want to offer support to someone who is suffering: "I learned very early on," he says, "that not everyone wants to talk, and you cannot take away someone else's pain. However, what you can do is to show them that you care, and that you are there, simply by being alongside."

Being alongside—what a simple but powerful way to show appreciation for someone. Andrew's point is that a hand on a shoulder and the offer of a cup of tea can be less intrusive and more supportive than a well-meaning "How are you feeling?" Allowing the person who is suffering to open up and talk when they want to, rather than when you feel they ought to, may be received with far more gratitude than premature encouragement to share feelings and talk.

building bridges

Appreciation goes deeper than a simple thank you. It is a heartfelt and slow-burning response to kindness. When we truly appreciate what someone has done for us, we are taking time to tune in more deeply to another human being's situation and motivation. The thanks goes beyond the joy of receiving and considers the giver's situation, too.

It may seem obvious, since most of us do it naturally, but we tend to overlook the fact that offering appreciation builds a bridge between two people that enables them to share key moments in life.

appreciating one another

It is easy to show appreciation:

• *"I really appreciated your beautiful/kind/unexpected/generous/ delightful gift. I can just imagine the trouble you went to in finding it."*

• *"I really appreciated your kind support during such a difficult time— especially as you have your own challenges at the moment."*

• *"I truly appreciate you coming with me today. I know how busy you are at the moment."*

• *"We so appreciate you sharing our day. I know many of you have traveled a very long way to be here."*

• *"I love and appreciate you for all that you have done for me during the course of my life. I know you have put aside many of your own plans for our benefit."*

job satisfaction

We spend more hours of our lives working than at any other activity—whether in paid work, as a volunteer, or as a big-hearted, long-suffering parent. Those who love what they do feel fulfilled and have a sense of well-being; those who are less than happy are more likely to feel discontented and resentful. Working with an attitude of gratitude does not mean allowing yourself to be taken for granted. Reciprocal gratitude is as important in the workplace as it is in our other relationships. The love of the task should never lead to exploitation. For example, everyone has the right to be paid fairly for the work that they do.

Job satisfaction tends to evolve as much through the positive relationships we build in the workplace as from the work itself. Therefore relationships, rather than money, influence stability in the workforce. The people with whom we work, whether alongside or remotely, help to give us a sense of belonging. Research suggests that

GRATITUDE IN PRACTICE:

In the workplace

Alex is a consultant who helps businesses to turn their finances around. He says, "There are no villains—or very rarely. When things go wrong it is usually because people have been trying to do their best, not their worst. However, over time what was previously the best way may no longer be the most effective way. Ultimately people tend to be full of gratitude for the opportunity to speak up about the problems they are facing, because they care a great deal and want things to turn out well."

those who feel appreciated by their boss, in particular, are less likely to be job-hunting. So it makes sense to do all you can to make your work environment a place driven by gratitude rather than blame, where people feel supported and appreciated rather than sidelined or overlooked.

Simple actions can make a big difference, such as acknowledging colleagues as you pass them in the corridor. You may not have time to stop and chat, but you are all part of the same community. Those in more junior roles or the service departments work hard but can be overlooked. And remember that senior colleagues are people too—not everyone is as confident as they appear. Saying thank you for the pay rise, the away day, the staff party, or a well-run meeting can help to offer validation and oil the wheels of strong management. Easiest of all: when the going gets tough, smile and say something positive. It will make everyone feel better about the task in hand.

a call to action

We tend to show appreciation for the things we attach most importance to. When we become focused primarily on ourselves and our own needs, the world loses balance. However, practicing gratitude consciously encourages us to connect with and feel grateful for the world around us. When we feel connected, we begin to notice more clearly what is going on—and to see when things are out of balance. Gratitude can therefore lead us to take action, to try to improve life not only for ourselves but also for others, because we begin to see very clearly that we are all part of the same universe. No man is an island.

Feeling grateful for your urban life, and all that your town or city has to offer, means that you are also more likely to tune in and care that the least well off are struggling, that levels of pollution are impacting on health, or that support is needed for young people who are out of work.

Although we have lost much of our connection with the earth and with wildlife, we are by nature conscious of the world around us and our place within it. If you love the natural world, how can you not be moved to despair at the sight of forest clearance, the impact of pollution, the devastation of animal species, and the destruction of so many natural resources?

Awareness and consciousness are not passive emotions. We cannot ignore those things that are out of balance once we have become aware of them. Gratitude can therefore become a powerful call for action—and a route to taking greater responsibility for our neighborhood, the environment, and the planet as a whole.

"Your energy will flow to where your attention goes."

Anonymous

"Your difficulties do not come to destroy you, but to help you to discover your hidden potential."

Adapted from a quote by A. P. J. Abdul Kalam (1931–2015),
11th President of India

redressing the balance

Not everything in life turns out as expected, and gratitude may be elusive in the early stages of tragedy or disaster, but gradually, with patience, a shift in perspective may occur.

As human beings we have a great capacity for compassion and empathy. When we see another's distress we may be moved to take action in appreciation of what they are experiencing. When a whole nation of hearts are moved by the sight of a refugee child in distress, the plight of a homeless family, news of a personal tragedy, or the devastation caused by an earthquake or tsunami, extraordinary changes can take place quite quickly. Instead of assuming that we are powerless, we start to believe that we can make a positive difference.

Good things happen when we put fear, prejudice, and our own problems to one side and start to feel grateful that we can contribute something of value. Only when we feel powerless do anger or depression and destruction follow.

Taking action in appreciation works best when the help offered is a genuine gift—one that is actually wanted and needed. We discover time and again that we feel good about ourselves when we are helping to "make things better." That is a beneficial side effect, but not the main goal. Operating from a position of self-regard and ego can lead to indebtedness and a sense of being beholden—literally "bound in gratitude." Showing gratitude and appreciation is at its most powerful when it stops being about "me" or "you"—and acknowledges that it is for the greater good of "us."

Horatio's garden

In Salisbury, England, there is a beautiful garden full of structural plants and striking sculptures. However, there are several unusual things about this garden:

• Its location. It is on a prime plot at the main district hospital: an oasis of calm that flourishes not far from the spinal treatment center, and within strolling distance of the visitor parking lots near by.

• Its conception: it was the brainchild of a very gifted and energetic young man called Horatio. A prospective medical student, he was only 17 when he spent a summer volunteering at the hospital, helping to feed and care for patients recovering from spinal injuries. He saw immediately that they needed somewhere to escape to, where they could relax and be themselves during their long recovery. After doing his research and gaining evidence of patients' needs and wishes, he used his initiative to lobby the chief executive with his idea.

• Sadly, there is a third reason that the garden is unusual. In a tragic accident, Horatio was attacked and killed by a polar bear while on a schools' expedition in Norway the following summer. That's not something any parent expects or can ever fully come to terms with.

The garden, by the award-winning designer Cleve West, is testament to an outpouring of gratitude for Horatio's energetic and vibrant young life, and appreciation for his inspired idea. Horatio's family were overwhelmed by the extraordinary wave of kindness and support received in the form of donations from those who had read the story of Horatio's death. Soon, his parents hope, there will be 11 Horatio's gardens at spinal units around Britain.

Although Horatio's story is on the website of his charity, Horatio's Garden, and woven into the fabric of the garden in Salisbury, it is humbling to see that the family's tragedy is not center stage. The focus of the organization is kept quite deliberately on the present-day patients and their recovery. Horatio's garden as a concept has taken off, and Horatio's legacy is one of recovery and remembrance—one that will be appreciated for generations.

"You have not lived today until you have done something for someone who can never repay you."

John Bunyan (1628–1688)

gratitude in action

If you would like some good ideas for putting appreciation into action you may like to start off with the ideas below, or by visiting one of the gratitude websites listed in the references on page 141.

whistle while you work

Does your work area reflect the time and effort that you put in to each working day? Many people have photographs of loved ones on their desktop to help to remind them of their greater motivation, but what about including symbols of gratitude for all that you do?

• Expand the gratitude culture. Do you take time to acknowledge a colleague who has something to celebrate? Do you take a moment to say thank you or to show your appreciation, even for the small things? Do you show appreciation publicly for great work and support? Never assume that no one will care or notice.

• Banish the whinge culture. Moans and groans can drag everyone down—even if they are delivered with wit and humor. What is your role in conversations? Do you roll with the mood or try to "look for the donkey" (see page 33), finding ways to evaluate and appreciate rather than denigrate?

• If someone shows you appreciation, do you savor the experience with gratitude and keep those flowers, that gift, the card, in plain sight—or do you tuck things away modestly in a drawer? Symbols of gratitude can help others to raise their game, too, and the whole team to feel valued.

• Do you feel grateful for your working environment? How much creative mess is good for your head? Some people's idea of order is a meticulously tidy workspace; others appreciate a bit of color and creativity. Does your work area feed stress or soothe it? How could you change it for the better?

• When is the last time you treated yourself to a plant, some flowers, or a picture for your desk?

• Practice forgiveness: it will help you. People will let you down. Awkward clients, late suppliers, and slow payers can all make life a misery. If someone has fallen short of their promises, ask them why. If they have caused you disruption, tell them so. Actively appreciating the way you feel and taking action to express your frustration in an open-minded and professional way will help you to create a more constructive dialogue. You may find the very person who was irritating you will feel grateful for the chance to explain what the problem was. If you hold on to feelings of anger, you will suffer more than they will.

• Make an effort to remember people's names—especially the names of those who are new to the organization. We all suffer from temporary amnesia from time to time but knowing the names of those you work alongside is an important sign that you value their presence and contribution.

making time for gratitude

There are a whole host of ways to show your appreciation for everyone and everything around you. The following ideas include suggestions to add to your gratitude journal, too.

"Feeling gratitude and not expressing it is like wrapping a present and not giving it."

William Arthur Ward (1921–1994), writer

the gift of praise

Take a moment to appreciate your family, friends, neighbors, and colleagues—honoring those who contribute to your world in the broadest sense:

• Who in your life deserves praise for something achieved or well done?

• What have you done that you can quietly praise yourself for?

• Is there someone in your community who deserves positive praise and feedback for all the hard work they put in, without much recognition?

directed gratitude

Sometimes in life we lose touch. Someone goes quiet. Often it is in the very moments that a friend, relative, or colleague seems to be most distant that he or she most needs your support and care. You can still offer your gratitude by focusing all your thoughts and attention on how much you care for and appreciate the person you are concerned about. The universe is made up of much more than we are aware of. It is not always wise to rely on logic and knowledge as the only means of offering support to one another.

take a journal moment

The following questions may take time and consideration to answer. Don't feel that you need to answer them instantly, or all at once. You could include them as questions in your gratitude journal—or may choose to revisit them from time to time each year.

• Who do you turn to during a time of turmoil?

• Who knows you better than you know yourself and loves you for who you are?

• Who tends to be there for you, no matter what?

• Who is your lifeline for the big stuff?

• Who keeps you sane with the little stuff?

• Who has made a difference to your life?

• Who has listened to your cares and worries without expecting anything in return?

• Who do you appreciate who does not always get shown appreciation?

• Who may be needing your support right now?

• Whom do you appreciate for the care they offer to others?

• Who would value you paying them greater attention, and cares when you are not around?

• How can you show someone close to you how much you care about and appreciate them?

Receiving gratitude at unexpected moments can have a very powerful impact. By taking a moment to send thanks, either actually—in a text, email, or phone call—or in your heart, you can add a burst of positivity or change the way your friend is facing their day.

When we know we are cared for and appreciated, we feel more empowered in our everyday lives. Receiving thanks has a positive impact and reminds us that we can make good things happen.

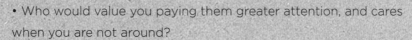

CHAPTER 6

sharing and thanksgiving

Every culture has traditions and festivals that involve sharing and celebration. From Thanksgiving to Christmas, Hanukkah to Diwali, Easter to Eid-al-Fitr, the Chinese Moon Festival to the Ghanaian Homowo Yam Festival, we have always given thanks for the harvest, for the seasons, for day and night, for our health and well-being, for spiritual nourishment, and for the food on our table.

Celebrating festivals, feasting, and spending time with those we love and care about all provide a sociable antidote to the fast pace of the twenty-first century. Old traditions offer us new ways of appreciating our abundant lives, as well as time-honored ways of offering thanks for all we hold dear.

festivals across the world

Giving thanks is embedded in the ceremonies of every spiritual tradition in the world. In early times, this may have involved more superstitious forms of worship, with forms of sacrifice and ritual that we would not embrace today, but nevertheless, recognizing that we are not alone is an important aspect of being human.

giving thanks, thanksgiving

An "attitude of gratitude" helps everyone to face the world in a positive and upbeat way, so it is no surprise that feelings of goodwill expand even farther when everyone gathers to celebrate and appreciate at the same time. Taking the time to be consciously aware of all that matters and to give thanks to those we love and care for—and even to those we find more challenging—is a great way to build bridges, reach joint understanding, and bring families and communities together. Thanksgiving helps us to move beyond petty differences and remember the wonder of life and what really matters to us all.

As every American will know, the Thanksgiving feast dates back to November 1621, when the newly arrived Pilgrims shared simple food with the local Wampanoag tribe. In Canada, Thanksgiving started even earlier, in 1578. It is credited to the English explorer Martin Frobisher, who with his men gave thanks for their safe return

to harbor after their expedition through the country's icy northern wastes to find the great Northwest Passage.

Since those early days, the annual tradition of sharing turkey, pumpkin pie, and other holiday treats has reunited families and friends across the whole continent.

"Gratitude is not only the greatest of virtues, but the parent of all the others."

Marcus Tullius Cicero (106–43 BCE), philosopher and theorist

Pumpkin Pie is made for sharing

Pumpkin pie is synonymous with beautiful Fall colors and seasonal hospitality. Every family has its own preferred recipe, and there is nothing more welcoming than being offered a thick slice of pie on a chilly October day.

Ingredients:

1 medium pumpkin, halved and seeds removed

2 eggs, plus an extra egg yolk

½ cup/170g/6oz soft brown sugar

1 heaped cup/115g/4oz superfine (caster) sugar

½ tsp salt

2 tsp cinnamon

1 tsp ground ginger

¼ tsp each ground nutmeg and ground cloves

¼ tsp ground cardamom (optional)

grated zest of half a lemon

1½ cups/12 fl oz heavy (double) cream (or a 12oz can unsweetened condensed milk)

1 sweet shortcrust ready-made pastry shell, 9 in. (23 cm) in diameter

Serves 8

Method:

1. Preheat the oven to 350°F/180°C/Gas 4.

2. First make the pumpkin purée: line a baking sheet with greaseproof paper or baking parchment. Place the pumpkin halves cut side down on the sheet and bake for 1–1½ hours, until the flesh is soft and can be easily pierced. Remove from the oven and allow to cool before scooping out the pulp. (For extra-smooth purée, push through a strainer/sieve before use.) Turn the oven up to 425°F/220°C/Gas 7.

3. Beat the eggs and egg yolk in a large bowl. Mix in the sugars, salt, spices, and lemon zest.

4. Add the pumpkin purée (making sure it is completely cool). Stir in the cream, and beat everything together until well mixed.

5. Pour the filling into the pastry shell, making sure it is spread nice and thickly (to allow for shrinkage as it cooks).

6. Bake for 15 minutes, then lower the temperature to 350°F/180°C/Gas 4 and bake for 45–55 minutes more.

7. To check whether the pie is ready, insert a skewer into the center of the filling. If it comes out clean, the pie is cooked. If not, bake for a few more minutes before testing again.

8. Leave the pie to cool and relax on a wire rack, then cut into slices. For extra decadence, serve with whipped cream, ice cream, or yogurt.

festivals of light

Light in a spiritual context is associated in every culture with the getting of enlightenment and the passing of night into day. It is a powerful symbol, whether represented by the peaceful flicker of candlelight or celebrated in a show of lights or noisy blaze of colorful fireworks.

Diwali (mid-October to mid-November, depending on the lunar year)
This festival of lights is a beautiful occasion and very important in the Hindu, Sikh, and Jain calendars. A festival of prayers and a day for exchanging sweets and goodwill, it is an official holiday in many countries. In the Hindu faith, Diwali uses light to symbolize the overcoming of ignorance that brings darkness to the world, and celebrates stepping toward the light of knowledge, understanding, and self-awareness. It marks the beginning of the lunar year and is a time for giving thanks for the triumph of good over evil. As part of the celebrations, hundreds of diyas (small earthenware lamps) are lit in doorways and windows.

Hanukkah (late December to early January)
This eight-day Jewish festival also marks the beginning of a new year, and it too uses light to symbolize thanksgiving and gratitude. Each of the eight candles in the Menorah is lit in a precise way and in a particular order each night of the festival, and burns for half an hour after nightfall.

breaking fast

Practicing the discipline of "going without" is seen in many traditions and practices as helpful for improving concentration and focus to help gain greater awareness and understanding.

Eid-al-Fitr (Festival of the Breaking of the Fast)
This festival in the Muslim calendar marks the end of Ramadan, an important time of prayer and fasting. Eid is celebrated on the first day of the month of Shawwāl. It is a day of prayer and forgiveness—and the only day when fasting is forbidden. On this day it is expected that as much charity as possible will be given, happily, to the poor and others in need.

Christmas (December 25)
Traditionally, Christmas Day also represented the breaking of a fast. In the Eastern Orthodox Church, fasting would continue throughout Advent, culminating in a strict fast on the eve of the Nativity (Christmas Eve). In the modern, secular world, many have moved away from this tradition, but the focus of thanksgiving still lies in the sharing of a meal with family, friends, and strangers.

Symbolic gifts

The gifts of the Magi in the Christmas story are familiar around the world:

Gold: a symbol of kingship, as well as being valuable currency.

Frankincense (olibanum): known for its distinctive scent, it can be seen as a symbol of anointment.

Myyrh: a valuable resin from the commiphora myyrha tree, myyrh was used for a breadth of medicinal purposes.

These symbolic gifts of health, wealth, and kingship have been replicated in different ways throughout time and cultures. Offering a gift that has symbolic value adds to its significance and meaning. (See page 52 and 109 for ideas on meaningful gifts that you can give.)

bring on the birthday

Birthdays are a wonderful time to show our appreciation. They have been celebrated with gifts at least since the time of the pharaohs in ancient Egypt, when astrologers needed to know details of date and time of birth in order to cast a horoscope for the leaders of the day, who were granted god-like status. Sharing the occasion of your birthday with others, and having them share theirs with you, is a wonderful way to celebrate each new age, as well as honoring life's transitions and rites of passage.

Parents the world over have baked or bought beautiful cakes to celebrate the birthdays of children (and adults) in the family. We are never too old to enjoy the fun of blowing out birthday candles and pausing to celebrate with friends.

Birthday celebrations, like so many festivals, are rooted in tradition and ancient history. In many cultures and traditions, birthdays are also closely linked to feast days and saints' days. The transition from childhood to adulthood is a particular milestone. In countries where Spanish and Portuguese influences are strong, young women of 15 are given a *Quinceañera*, to honor the transition from girlhood to womanhood. (As part of the Quinceañera in some regions, the person whose birthday it is will pass 15 candles to the 15 people who have supported them during their life's journey so far—and to symbolize the years they are now leaving behind.) In Brazil there is the *fest de debutante*. In the USA and Canada, sweet sixteen parties are popular. Elsewhere, eighteenth and twenty-first birthdays celebrate the official "coming of age," with all the freedom, independence, and responsibility that it represents.

From first birthday to last birthday, most people relish receiving birthday cards too. In the UK anyone who reaches the age of 100 receives a card sent on the behalf of Queen Elizabeth II.

birthday gifts that give

• The next time you have a birthday to celebrate, consider giving gifts to others instead of waiting to receive them!

• Instead of giving gifts to each other, consider giving time or money to a humanitarian cause or a welfare organization.

• Pass on a gift that has had meaning for you in the past: perhaps you were given a piece of jewelry, a book, a pen, or an ornament for a significant birthday, which you love but no longer use. Do you know someone who is the same age as you were then who would enjoy it?

Celebrating good times and great memories

We are so fortunate to be living in an age where it is possible to share photos, stories, and memories so widely and so quickly.

"I create a photographic calendar each year as a Christmas present for the family, which records key moments of the year (and includes everyone's birthdays, too!). The grandparents really appreciate it and always look forward to it." Sue

"For my daughter's 21st birthday I created a photo record of her life with captions and stories. She loved it and was so grateful as it reminded her of her early days." Nicole

"My father was a very talented artist, though very modest about his skills. I decided to have a number of his pictures turned into cards. We have had so much positive feedback that I am going to create some more." Phil

gratitude through remembrance

It may seem strange to be including farewells in a section on festivals and celebrations, but, as anyone who has lost someone dear to them will know, we also have a deep human need to show our gratitude to those who are no longer present with us on this earth. A funeral planned with heart can be a beautiful occasion, even though it is full of sadness. A careful choice of flowers, music, words, and tributes can make the difference between a cold, soulless occasion and one that leads to a sense of connection among those present while providing comfort during a period of grief. Saying goodbye with grace and forgiveness soothes the soul and helps us to support one another and to adapt to the future.

Try asking yourself the following questions, (perhaps via your journal pages):

• How has this person helped to make me who I am today?

• How can I best give thanks for who they were and all they did?

• How can I make a contribution that honors them and offers grateful remembrance?

• Which places, what food, what music, what scents, what flowers remind me of them?

precious memories

It can be cathartic to commit to paper or to screen, in your journal, all the things you have to be grateful for and all the things you appreciated about someone who is no longer so materially present in your life. It may help you to sense that they are still a part of your life in an important way, and to celebrate all that they meant to you.

I have learned four valuable things about grief:

• That when sadness wells up, be grateful for the tears and feel the sorrow deeply, so that the bright memories are etched all the more deeply into your heart.

• That "this too shall pass"—perhaps not today, or tomorrow, or next week, but in time something will shift so that we are left with gratitude, rather than pain.

• That laughter is cathartic. It has the power to change your mood instantly, and to increase the opportunity for joy. Sharing a simple joke can be just enough to remind you that it is okay to laugh, and that it is possible to be happy and to miss someone at the same time.

• To be patient—with yourself and others—and to accept that grief affects everyone differently, sometimes at unexpected times and in surprising ways.

Facing transition

The psychiatrist Elisabeth Kübler-Ross was one of the first people to identify that any form of grief, loss, or momentous change tends to trigger the following emotions at one point or another: Denial, Anger, Bargaining, Depression, Acceptance. These are not linear states of being. In some circumstances we get stuck at a particular stage; in others we jump straight from one state to another. Focusing consciously on reasons for feeling gratitude can help us to find a constructive pathway through the darker times and to reach acceptance in whatever form that takes. In the quiet moments we transform, and through gratitude for what has been we gradually turn into the people we are yet to become. It is the chrysalis effect.

GRATITUDE IN PRACTICE:

Compassion in action

Earlier this year the BBC (UK) ran a news story about a former German soldier called Heinrich Steinmeyer, who had been captured in France at the age of 19 during the Second World War. He was removed to Cultybraggan, a prisoner-of-war camp near to Comrie village in Perthshire, Scotland, and stayed there from November 1944 until June 1945. He was relocated twice before being released in 1948.

A young man from a poor background, Steinmeyer was enrolled in the Hitler Youth and was a member of the notorious Waffen SS at the time of his capture. He would have considered the British people his enemy.

However, much to his surprise, he found himself in the heart of a community that had the grace to treat him with kindness. He was befriended by local schoolchildren who got chatting to him through the fence of the prison, one of whom eventually became his wife. He stayed on in Scotland after the war, developing firm friendships with those he had come to know.

His story hit the news headlines because following his death at the age of 90, it was revealed that Steinmeyer had left his savings of £384,000 to "the elderly" in the village in Perthshire where he had been held prisoner.

His will stated: "Herewith, I would like to express my gratitude to the people of Scotland for the kindness and generosity that I have experienced in Scotland during my imprisonment of war and hereafter."

gratitude in action

Although holidays and birthdays provide set times to celebrate and be grateful, remember that you can celebrate at any time of year.

host a celebration—large or small

Whatever kind of shared celebration you are planning, it does not have to be stressful. Remember that gratitude is all about sharing the load, so here are a few things to keep in mind:

1. Instead of planning for "perfect," aim to "expect—and accept—the unexpected!"

2. Accept with gratitude as much help on the day as your kitchen can accommodate.

3. Put yourself first at a key point in the day, so that you have showered and dressed and are feeling relaxed with plenty of time to spare.

On the more practical side of things, here are a few tips to get you started:

• Be prepared! Planning prevents last-minute stresses and headaches, and it can help to make a reverse timeline, working back to when you need to start—which may be a few days in advance.

• Serving dishes, crockery, flatware (cutlery), and glasses all need to be sourced—and washed. Making sure you have the extras you need, such as table napkins, candles, and candleholders, well in advance can help the day to go smoothly. Remember that flowers do not have to be lavish to add joy—colored leaves, twigs, berries, and foliage can be just as arresting as a spectacular bouquet. There is nothing like having visitors to provide a good excuse to clean your home and tidy everything up. Getting it all done can be very liberating!

• It is a good idea to set the table the evening before (and, if you have a pet or a small child with curious fingers, keep everything lightly covered and protected).

• When it comes to the food, stick to your favorite recipes. Experienced cooks always advise against experimenting with a new recipe when you are hosting a large crowd. If you're stuck for ideas for desserts and vegetables, get the word out and accept suggestions—or buy ready-made.

• Do as much as possible ahead of time, by planning the menu well in advance and preparing as much food beforehand as you can. There is much to be said for not being too proud to buy in some dishes to ease your way—especially those you are less confident about making.

• Don't try to provide everything yourself, though. A gathering where everyone has contributed is always remembered warmly, and it shares the strain of preparation and the pressure of the expense. So let friends and family bring things: find out what people are good at and embrace the art of delegating. Make sure that the person who is bringing appetizers is a reliable sort who always turns up early; and entrust the "nice to have but not essential" dishes to those who have a tendency to turn up late (or not at all)—such as cheese, desserts, etc. Involve the children, if you can. They can decorate the table, put out nibbles, or prepare a fruit salad—and it will make the day more special for them.

Remember: Relax, enjoy, give thanks

• Refreshments should be planned in advance, too—once everyone has a drink in their hand, they won't mind waiting for the meal. Make sure you provide plenty of non-alcoholic drinks, too.

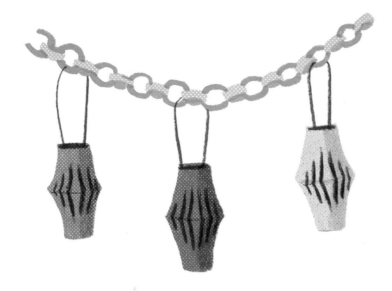

• Chilling the glasses in the fridge or freezer gives them a dramatic frosted appearance and helps to keep the drinks cool.

• Too much formality can prevent people from relaxing. If you are serving a large meal, you don't need to worry about exotic canapés. Your guests will be grateful just to have something simple to go with their drinks while they have a chat.

• Try to relax! One of the joys of involving other people is that no one minds too much when things don't go quite to plan—and there is always an alternative solution on offer. Whether a power cut ruins your dessert or you overcook the turkey, it really doesn't matter. The meal may be the centerpiece, but people have come mainly to relax and to enjoy one another's company.

• Finally, be thankful. Remember to pause and give thanks for everyone—right here, right now. These occasions are precious, fun, and always to be remembered.

making time for gratitude

I am thinking of you

Have you ever received a gift or a gesture out of the blue? Do you remember how it made you feel? Unexpected gifts as gestures of kindness and support can be the most memorable, uplifting, and heartwarming of all.

A simple posy of flowers, a care parcel in the form of tea and cake, an invitation to lunch, a text, or a phone call: there are numerous ways to reach out spontaneously to show our friends how much we care about them. Receiving a card unexpectedly from someone you haven't heard from for a long time can really make your day.

• Do you know someone who is going through a difficult time, who could do with an act of kindness or some moral support?

• Do you want to let someone know you are thinking about them?

• Is there someone in your life who has been generous or supportive without expecting anything in return?

• Who needs you to share some goodwill with them today?

> *"Hope smiles from the threshold of the year to come, whispering 'it will be happier'..."*
>
> Alfred, Lord Tennyson (1809–1892)

embracing good fortune

Gratitude is a cornerstone of every ancient faith and belief system, from the beliefs of First Nation aboriginal peoples who offer thanks to earth and sky, for the seasons, and to the creatures who share this planet, to those who embrace suffering as a pathway to gratitude and spiritual freedom, and those who have an alternative practice of prayer and contemplation. Whenever we find a way to embrace our good fortune and live life with an open heart, so our appreciation of the joy, fun, and delight of life increases. When we can share in the success and happiness of others and be joyful for our friends and those we love, we find it easier to be spontaneously happy and embrace the joy of being alive. Take a moment to give thanks for yourself as well as for others.

gratitude blessing

The blessing on the following page has been inspired by the Buddhist practitioner Jack Kornfield. Jack Kornfield is known around the world as a Buddhist practitioner and teacher. His many books are highly respected and his website is a rich source of ideas for meditation practice. His work consistently explains the rich value that such practice offers us in developing a more open-hearted, joyful, and grateful approach to life.

Blessing of gratitude

Let yourself sit quietly and in a relaxed fashion. Take a deep breath and then let go. Let your heart feel easy. Listen to your breath as you breathe in and out quietly and naturally. Allow your body to let go of all tension and become ready to receive this blessing:

I offer my gratitude to the universe and all that is in it, for
the friends I have been given;
the family I have been given;
the joy of life that I have been given;
the state of health and well-being that I have been given;
the neighbors that I have been given;
the teachers that I have been given;
the wisdom that I have been given;
the beauty of this earth, and the animals and birds that we have
all been given;
my life and all that I have been given.

Now continue to breathe in and out gently. Picture someone you care about, and think about them as they go about their daily life—and about the happiness and success you wish for them. With each breath, offer them your thanks from the bottom of your heart:

May you always have joy in your heart.
May you always enjoy good fortune.
May your happiness continue to increase.
May you always have peace and well-being on this earth.

CHAPTER 7

seeking contentment

Living a life of gratitude is both incredibly simple and, on occasion, extremely challenging—and sometimes both at the same time.

The challenges occur because we have a tendency to hold on tightly to negative emotions, such as resentment, anger, and fear that prevent us from feeling wholehearted gratitude and contentment. The simplicity lies in the realization that once we let go of those feelings and recognize the power and beauty of acceptance, it is possible for the barriers to gratitude to fade away.

what is contentment?

Contentment is defined as a state of happiness and peaceful satisfaction. Seeking contentment is about having "enough." We feel grateful for what we have without hungering for more. Instead of a sense of entitlement, a kind of faith develops that we will be provided for. Sometimes having enough and feeling contented can mean living modestly—but at its heart it is more about trust, about believing that there is "more than enough to go round."

Why, then, when we have so much to be grateful for, do we spend so much time complaining, regretting, or wishing? The clue may lie in our sense of entitlement. It leaves us wanting, expecting, and disappointed, by contrast with having enough, which guides us to a place of gratitude and trust.

Can it be that in modern times, when so many of us live in relative comfort (compared to previous generations), we have come to expect certain things as our right? When these are lacking, we feel that we have been deprived in some way, rather than noticing all that we have and appreciating the gift. A sense of entitlement provides very little space for gratitude to flourish because it is self-orientated. There is no giving and receiving, there is only taking. We lack balance.

"Wear gratitude like a cloak and it will sustain every corner of your life."

Rumi (1207–1273), poet and mystic

In a culture of acquisition we will always feel that we are entitled to more (bigger bonuses, greater bandwidth, faster cars, more exotic holidays), and that we can never have enough. Ultimately this lack of exchange can lead to loneliness and a feeling of being separate from the rest of the world. In a very real sense, our cultural sense of entitlement is upsetting the balance of the entire natural world.

"Count your blessings (instead of sheep)."

Irving Berlin, 1954

the danger of entitlement

Much of the discontent and unhappiness we feel in life is connected to the things we do not have. When we compare our own situation with other people's we will always be left wanting—not least because we don't know the full picture. We don't really know what anyone else's life is actually like.

However, the magic is that disappointment and dissatisfaction are not always negative; they can also become a driving force that leads us to strive and to achieve. By taking stock when we feel negative, we can choose to focus on gratitude in the form of feeling thankful for future possibilities instead. Once we acknowledge that we have choice in our lives, we also realize that we can bring about change. For example, not earning enough to buy the house of your dreams might lead you to come up with a strategy for co-purchase or to choose to rent somewhere beautiful instead. Being unhappy in a relationship may lead to a re-evaluation of your actions and choices—and the decision to try to work on things together rather than blame each other or walk away.

When we expect less and appreciate more, something interesting happens: levels of satisfaction about small things become higher. The child who has strived to improve on a D grade is thrilled with their C and starts to see a B as possible; the person who earns very little appreciates every penny of a performance bonus and has faith in their prospects for the future. Letting go of the idea that we are entitled and swapping it for a feeling of appreciation is a powerful step toward inner contentment and happiness.

GRATITUDE IN PRACTICE:

Giving away the past

"I love my books and had built up a substantial collection—many from college and school days," says Tammy. "The idea of giving any of them away was anathema to me. They were part of who I am—or so I thought. When I came to move home in my fifties I started to browse through some of the books as I packed them. I realized that not only was the typeface far too small for my aging eyes, it was also the first time I had leafed through the pages in 30 years! I decided to take radical action before I had a chance to change my mind. I photographed the books' spines so I could re-order favorite titles online, and took several boxes of books to goodwill stores. The charity volunteers were grateful to have such a useful windfall, my husband was grateful that our removal storage charges would not be quite as high, and as an added bonus our grandchildren were very proud that I had finally discovered the joy of reading books online and had made it into the twenty-first century. A positive result all round."

feeling gratitude for our friends

One area where we are rarely left wanting is in the field of friendship. As the saying goes, "friends are the family that we choose for ourselves." We know we are blessed with the friends whom we invite into our life—they make us laugh, they comfort and support us through the tough times, they remind us of who we are and what life is all about. Finding ways to offer thanks to those we hold most dear is a joy and a privilege, and we must do it as often and as much as possible!

There is a truism that each moment of life is lived forward but tends to be understood backward. When we think back to times past, we may have favorite memories—of precious moments, of places we have seen, experiences we have had, our successes, our losses, and, as we get older, perhaps sharing our life with someone special, marriage, or the birth of children or grandchildren. We savor fond recollections of friendship and companionship, and are more likely to appreciate what has gone before—and to view misunderstandings with compassion and increased perspective.

making amends

Most families and friends experience misunderstandings from time to time, but sometimes these transform into full-blown estrangement. Years may pass without contact, until no one really understands why the disagreement happened any more. Each "side" waits for the other to take the first step toward forgiveness, and meanwhile each has a lesser life without the other in it.

As human beings we are remarkable. We have free will and the power of conscious choice. We can choose our responses. Every one of us has the power to create change within ourselves, and to reach out to others to put things right. Making amends requires someone to make a positive choice—to risk a moment of rejection by putting another person's needs before their own. The chances are that once you have reached out, even if there is a period of unsettled adjustment, there will be a reciprocal sense of gratitude that you have been in contact and that a bridge has been built.

Nurturing understanding

Has someone upset you, or caused disruption in your life? If you put yourself in their shoes for a moment, does it alter your perspective? Can you find it within yourself to see the world through a new lens and let go of the negativity? When we hold on to irritation with other people, ultimately we are often causing more disruption to ourselves than to them.

The role of forgiveness

Has someone in your life caused you pain or distress? Has your own behavior caused you a problem that you find it hard to forgive yourself for? When we hold on to negative feelings, they hurt us more than they hurt the person or event that we feel negative about. By digging deep and finding a way to accept your feelings, it becomes possible to start to transform them into something more constructive. Accepting the past and offering forgiveness either actually or privately, in your own heart, is an important step toward living life with gratitude—for the understanding of what has been and the awareness that it offers. In time we can learn to forgive, and to feel grateful for the greater understanding we have developed.

gratitude through fulfillment

Those who know what it is to become a parent for the first time understand the overwhelming sense of wonder, love, and gratitude that having a baby son or daughter can generate—and how that bond produces a sense of love and fulfillment through the ups and downs of life. For others, the experience of creating, developing, or contributing through work may lead to a powerful sense of accomplishment and happiness. Gratitude for our own contentment generates kindness toward others. When we feel a sense of belonging, we want to keep everyone safe and make sure their needs are met.

A feeling of gratitude may lead a new parent to make a donation to a favorite cause, or buy gifts in honor of their child; a successful businessperson is moved to develop a philanthropic trust or focus on developing improved terms and conditions for their employees.

The moments when we feel most connected and of greatest value to others also give us our greatest sense of belonging and self-worth. The light in our own lives makes us feel more generous and grateful toward the world at large.

paying it forward

Feeling gratitude for our work and the pathway to learning helps us to become aware of where we are on the bigger path. Those who live life with a generous heart learn that if we give to others with no expectation of receiving in return, we are more likely to receive unexpected trust, loyalty, and other heartfelt benefits.

The business coach Bev James has embraced this philosophy throughout her career. She has offered sound advice freely, she has given away information on her website at no cost, and she looks after her friends, family, and colleagues with generosity. Over time her business has grown and expanded. She makes no distinction between her well-known clients and those who have slowly furrowed their own path. Bev always pays it forward and trusts that the rewards will follow. She has never been wrong about that: the power of gratitude has its own rewards, and those she has helped have always willingly given back in exchange.

• When someone asks you for a favor, how do you feel?

• Do you offer your time and knowledge willingly, with good heart?

• Is there someone you could help today with no expectation of reward?

• Has someone offered you support, help, or guidance at some time, simply out of the kindness of their heart?

Taking time to offer them thanks, whether actually or in your heart—or in your journal—will help to cement the feeling of contentment and connectedness. When we appreciate that we are all part of the same whole, we see very clearly that giving to others is exactly the same as giving to ourselves.

GRATITUDE IN PRACTICE:

Looking fear in the face

On the afternoon of October 9, 2012, Malala Yousafzai was taking her usual bus home from school in Pakistan when she was shot in the head. She had been targeted as punishment for writing about life under the Taliban in a public blog, which had been publicized by the BBC in Britain. She recovered from her injuries, and has since then been given several prestigious awards, including the Nobel Peace Prize. She is now appreciated and respected everywhere as an ambassador for peace. There are hundreds of women around the world who are grateful for her courage and her example.

your life as legacy

It is natural to want to be remembered warmly and with gratitude when we leave school, a place of work, a neighborhood—and ultimately this earth. Most people, as they get older, give some thought to their legacy. However, sometimes we become so focused on the destination that we forget to be thankful for what we have learned along the way.

Modesty is an admirable trait, but not when it diminishes life and makes everything invisible. Looking toward the future with gratitude and focused intention helps us to make our lives feel more worthwhile in the present moment.

• What can you be grateful for that you would like others to share in and to benefit from?

• What are the "lessons in life" that you would like to share so that others have the chance to see life through your eyes?

• Where have you traveled and what have you seen that might fascinate and interest future generations?

• What mistakes have you made that you are grateful for because you have learned from them, and that others might learn from too?

• Which people in your life have had a positive impact on you, whose memory you would like to keep alive?

• Who would you like to share these memories with so that they can benefit the next generation, too?

gratitude guru: **David Steindl-Rast**

"Stop. Look. Go. That's all."

David Steindl-Rast (1926–)

No book on gratitude is complete without mentioning David Steindl-Rast OSB, an Austrian-born Catholic Benedictine monk with a peaceful and mesmeric voice, who cofounded a center for spiritual studies in 1968 with teachers from the Buddhist, Sufi, Hindu, and Jewish faiths. Brother David also cofounded the nonprofit A Network for Grateful Living, which is dedicated to gratefulness as a route to transformation in all societies. His videos and talks are an inspirational joy for everyone who is on a mission to live life more thankfully (see Resources, page 141).

Success and gratitude

It is very important to stop and take a moment to acknowledge life's milestones. How can we stride forward with clarity unless we know where we are in relation to where we began—and give thanks for getting to this point?

The following symbols of success and gratitude also represent important rites of passage:

Medals and trophies—Usually hard-won, they represent a moment when striving for personal goals and competing against the best delivers wonderful results, and they are received with gratitude. Olympians compete for the glory of winning, not for riches. They represent the appreciation and admiration of a nation. We, too, are usually more motivated by personal progress than by the material comforts that come in the wake of success.

Birthdays—Not always welcomed as we get older, they are nevertheless important. They are symbolic celebrations that represent rites of passage—each year of our life and the love, appreciation, and gratitude that others have for our presence on this earth. The gifts, cards, and tokens received and the way in which we celebrate help us to focus consciously on our gratitude for the past and present, as well as energizing our hopes and expectations for the future.

Examination results—of every sort. They represent the gratitude that you might choose to show to your teachers for taking you to this point, to your parents for supporting you, and to yourself for your achievements. If the grades are less than you had hoped for, there is reason to be grateful that you have more potential, and that the best is yet to come.

honoring good times

How often do you pause to celebrate life's key moments? Some people and some families are very good at marking life's milestones with a special meal, a gift, or a mention that shows gratitude for what has happened and honors those involved. Others shrug off the moment with modesty and a reluctance to fuss. Thinking consciously about the life we live at any moment, and focusing with conscious gratitude on all the positive elements, can help us to adjust our course so that every minute counts. We are more likely to stop doing the things that take us away from our destination, and move toward doing more of those things that we want our legacy to be about. Contentment evolves from the knowledge that whatever the material outcome, yours has been a life well lived.

Remember:
Appreciate
thankfully

gratitude happy-tude

Sometimes we spend so much time measuring personal happiness against other people's achievements or expectations that we overlook the joys we already have. There is a profound connection between gratitude and contentment.

List three things that make you want to shout out in happiness (or at the very least always make you smile):

1.
_____
_____

2.
_____
_____

3.
_____
_____

gratitude in action

light a candle

Has someone you cared about died recently? Have you parted from someone you care about? Perhaps you have been separated temporarily by work or geographical distance? Lighting a candle in remembrance or as a tribute is a very simple symbol of gratitude for the light and energy that others bring to our life. A single candle can shine a light that is brighter than its flame, with an intensity that matches the strongest and most sincere of feelings.

Meditating on a single flame is a powerful way to concentrate our innermost thoughts. It helps us to enter a frame of mind in which we feel able to offer thanks for all that is sacred, to be grateful for the continued well-being of our loved ones, or to make sense of our feelings and our memories.

Light your candle in silence, and take a moment to focus peacefully and completely on the person you are thinking of. If you are able to play some music that reflects your mood, the intensity will be increased as more of your senses will be involved in the tribute. Breathe slowly and consciously, while saying or thinking whatever comes to mind in farewell, sorrow, appreciation, or remembrance.

how do I want to be remembered?

A page in your journal? A mind map? A wall of ideas and pictures? There are many ways to tap into your creative mind and soul to visualize and give shape to your innermost wishes. Over time you can collect ideas and pictures for your journal or create them as a collage. By capturing them and giving them visual form you will help to give them meaning and bring them to life.

my gratitude challenge

This one needs time to think about and plan. Many people who have taken up a large-scale challenge have done so because they want to give back in some way or to offer support. We all know people who have taken action to walk, run, swim, climb, or skydive, or who have undertaken some other tremendous feat for the benefit of a cause. Choosing a challenge for the good of others has the benefit of helping other people to get the "feel-good factor" by helping you, sponsoring you, and sharing in the glory of your success. The impact can be personally transformative, too.

"I climbed Mount Kilimanjaro to celebrate my 60th birthday and to test my resilience, while also raising money for my local hospital. On the trip I also happened to meet the man who would become my husband, which was a joy-filled bonus!" Vanda

"I wanted to challenge myself by running a half-marathon and it was the perfect way to raise funds for the hospice that cared for our family friend, Aunty Margaret, too. The training was tough, but I loved taking part in the event and am ready to train for my next event now!" Libby

Is there something you could undertake for a good cause? Try sitting with the idea for a little while. You will know when it is right for you to take action.

your gratitude portrait

Liz Handy is a talented photographer who has developed an interesting way of creating self-portraits. She invites her subjects to select six objects that define different areas of their life, plus a flower. Your gratitude portrait has a similar mission, with a slight twist: the objects you choose must be things that represent the areas of your life, or the people, that you value and are grateful for.

To start your own gratitude portrait, ask yourself, or write in your journal:

• Which three people in my life have I learned the most from, and why?

• Which two people (outside my immediate family) need me the most today?

• Which author/artist/poet/musician/engineer/scientist have I always admired without taking the time to explore or enjoy his/her work? Start today!

making time for gratitude

Focusing on your relationships with others—and yourself—with gratitude can help pave the way to contentment. Contemplating these areas of your life can add focus to your journal entries too:

treasured friendships

Take a moment to honor and focus on your friends.

• Think about them one at a time—what they look like, how they smile and laugh, a key moment that you have shared together.

• If you were to move home or leave school/college/your job tomorrow, who would you want to contact to thank for the part they played in your life?

• Who would you like to leave a "legacy letter" for—to offer gratitude and encouragement for their future?

finding peace

Contentment comes from knowing that you have made peace with those to whom you caused pain, or that you have found a way to let go of past hurts and disappointments so that you can embrace your future with a thankful heart.

• Who have you fallen out of contact with, whom you still miss and remember from a time now past?

• If you are unable to reconnect with them or express your appreciation for their part in your life, what would you have liked to say to them in gratitude? Writing a letter, composing a verse, or creating something in gratitude can really help us to make peace with the past.

• Is there someone you need to let go of and forgive, in order to be free to live your life in a new way?

offering gratitude for who you are right now

How can we better appreciate who we are in order to transform ourselves into what we can become? Can discontent or disappointment about something in your past be transformed into acceptance, or recharged in a way that helps you to let go and move forward? The science of happiness and research into gratitude suggests that it can.

Scientists tell us that it is impossible to feel genuinely positive about something at the same time as feeling negative. We can transform our negative feelings by accepting that they exist and choosing to overlay them with a new and more positive outlook. Nurturing thankfulness for all that we have can be re-energizing and enough to drive us forward with creative change. It is forgiveness in action.

• Take a moment to give thanks for the way you see the world: your senses, your thoughts, your choices, your actions.

• Allow yourself to appreciate all the qualities you have—and those you would like to enhance and improve.

• Think back over your life and think of three things that you are proud of.

• Think of one thing that you feel regretful or unhappy about.

• Consider your future and one thing you would value doing more of. Can you put in place a plan or steps to make that happen?

• If you were to write yourself a thank-you message, what would you say? (No negatives allowed!)

"It is through gratitude for the present moment that the spiritual dimension of life opens up."

Eckhart Tolle (1948–), author and spiritual teacher

Quiz: *How grateful is your attitude?*

On a scale of 0 to 10, where are you on the Gr-Attitude scale now? Try this quiz to get an overview of your approach to gratitude, and find out in which areas you could increase your gratitude or appreciation.

1. I look forward to each new day:

No					Sometimes					Yes
0	1	2	3	4	5	6	7	8	9	10

2. I try to look for the positive in every situation:

No					Sometimes					Yes
0	1	2	3	4	5	6	7	8	9	10

3. I prefer to think the best of people:

No					Sometimes					Yes
0	1	2	3	4	5	6	7	8	9	10

4. I find it easy to offer help to others:

No					Sometimes					Yes
0	1	2	3	4	5	6	7	8	9	10

5. I find it easy to accept help from others:

No					Sometimes					Yes
0	1	2	3	4	5	6	7	8	9	10

6. I would help a stranger who was in need:

No					Perhaps					Yes
0	1	2	3	4	5	6	7	8	9	10

7. I often actively feel grateful for my friends and/or my family:

No					Sometimes					Yes
0	1	2	3	4	5	6	7	8	9	10

8. There is so much in the world that is beautiful and to be thankful for:

No					Perhaps					Yes
0	1	2	3	4	5	6	7	8	9	10

9. I own everything I need to be happy:

No					Perhaps					Yes
0	1	2	3	4	5	6	7	8	9	10

10. Generally in life, I feel very contented:

No					Sometimes					Yes
0	1	2	3	4	5	6	7	8	9	10

Mostly 7–10 scores

Feeling thankful comes easily to you. Did you score 10/10 on many of these questions? Your levels of gratitude will shore up your life with resilience and perseverance and help you to feel happier every day.

Mostly 4–6 scores

Do you live life with a touch of cynicism? Do you prioritize work over spending time with your friends and family? It is possible that you are shutting out companionship and support that could enrich your life and make you happier.

Any 0–3 scores

Sometimes in life we become so overwhelmed with our troubles that we feel stuck and alone. If any of your scores are on the low side, please seek support from a friend or from a professional who could help you to shine a new light on your situation. There is much to feel grateful for in this evolving world of ours.

"Do not spoil what you have by desiring what you have not; remember that what you now have was once among the things you only hoped for."

Epicurus (341–270 BCE)

conclusion

a life of gratitude

Conscious gratitude leads to contentment. Over time, it feeds the memory of a life well lived.

When we are grateful for the beauty and variety of the world around us, we start to want to protect rather than destroy it.

When we appreciate one another's differences, we start to celebrate those differences and welcome the contrast, rather than expecting everyone to be the same.

When we stop regretting and start accepting, we start to live in a way that is more loving and realistic—and cast ourselves in a role where we cease to be victims of the past and start to make positive choices for the future.

When we break the habit of negative self-talk and become grateful for who we are, we start to see the future more positively and enjoy our unique place in the world.

When we are able to spot the reasons to be grateful in any situation, we step nearer to grace and to peace. Gratitude is, quite simply, the route to happiness.

Make time to count your blessings—every day.

references

All quotations included in the book remain © copyright of the authors and are acknowledged as follows:

Page 18 Oprah Winfrey, "What Oprah Knows for Sure about Gratitude," from *O, The Oprah Magazine*, November 2012, www.oprah.com/spirit/oprahs-gratitude-journal-oprah-on-gratitude

Page 29 S. L. Kerr, A. O'Donovan, & C. A. Pepping (2015), *Journal of Happiness Studies* 16: 17. doi:10.1007/s10902-013-9492-1

Page 71 Robert A. Emmons, *Thanks: How the New Science of Gratitude Can Make You Happier*, Houghton Mifflin, 2007

Page 72 As heard on BBC Radio 2

Page 76 Pilar Godino, *The Business Alchemist: In pursuit of the soul of leadership*, Hay House, 2013

Page 83 John F. Kennedy, "Proclamation 3560—Thanksgiving Day, 1963," November 5, 1963. Quoted by Gerhard Peters and John T. Woolley, *The American Presidency Project*, www.presidency.ucsb.edu/ws/?pid=9511

Pages 88–89 Algoe, Sara B., Shelly L. Gable, and Natalya C. Maisel, "It's the Little Things: Everyday Gratitude as a Booster Shot for Romantic Relationships," *Personal Relationships*, 2010, available at www.sciencedaily.com/releases/2010/05/100524072912.htm. See also www.saraalgoe.com/bio

Pages 96–97 Visit www.horatiosgarden.org.uk to watch a video of the garden

Page 100 William Arthur Ward, quoted at www.goodreads.com/quotes/189187-feeling-gratitude-and-not-expressing-it-is-like-wrapping-a

Pages 104–105 Adapted from Elise Bauer's "Old Fashioned Pumpkin Pie" recipe, and acknowledged with thanks: www.simplyrecipes.com/recipes/suzannes_old_fashioned_pumpkin_pie/

Page 112 www.bbc.co.uk/news/uk-scotland-tayside-central-38184935; www.scotsman.com/lifestyle/interview-heinrich-steinmeyer-former-pow-1-476058

Page 118 A more complete meditation by Jack Kornfield can be found at "Meditation on Gratitude and Joy." www.jackkornfield.com/meditation-gratitude-joy

Page 129 David Steindl-Rast, "Stop. Look. Go," a video on the Gratefulness.org website: www.gratefulness.org/blog/delighted-share-new-video-stop-look-go. On the same website you will find "My Private Gratitude Journal," an easy and inspiring way to get started: www.gratefulness.org/practice

Page 135 Eckhart Tolle, "Eckhart Tolle on the Beauty of Today," in *O, The Oprah Magazine*, May 2010

further resources

From books, to videos, to websites, to ideas for evolution!

inspiring books and videos

Schwartzberg, Louie, "Nature, Beauty, Gratitude," (featuring David Steindl-Rast), TED, 2011, www.ted.com/talks/louie_schwartzberg_nature_beauty_gratitude

Seligman, Martin E.P., *Learned Optimism: How to Change Your Mind and Your Life*, Vintage, 2006

Simon-Thomas, Emiliana R., "Compassion in the Brain," YouTube, September 25, 2013, www.youtube.com/watch?v=Ie4htPTeOvA

Soul Pancake, "An Experiment in Gratitude: The Science of Happiness," July 11, 2013, www.youtube.com/watch?v=oHv6vTKD6lg

Steindl-Rast, David, "Want to Be Happy? Be Grateful," TED, 2013, www.ted.com/talks/david_steindl_rast_want_to_be_happy_be_grateful

Trice, Laura, "Remember to Say Thank You," TED, 2008, www.ted.com/playlists/206/give_thanks

practical resources and websites

Exercises, questionnaires, and experiments in gratitude:

Authentic Happiness
The Penn State University website offers a range of questionnaires on gratitude, happiness, and other measures of well-being. You can take part too, by following this link: www.authentichappiness.sas.upenn.edu

The Franciscan Spiritual Center, "Musings on Gratitude"
www.fscaston.org/musings-on-gratitude

The Greater Good Science Center at the University of Berkeley
The University of Berkeley is at the forefront of current research into gratitude and its impact on our lives. Its website is a rich source of information: www.greatergood.berkeley.edu

The Happier Human
A generous-minded soul called Amit Amin has created the Happier Human website, a collection of personal musings and extensive resources: www.happierhuman.com

The Ripple Revolution
Curt Rosengren's Ripple Revolution website offers many routes to retuning our mindset to positive. This experiment is specifically focused on gratitude and is something any of us could do to great power and effect: www.ripplerevolution.com/would-this-gratitude-experiment-make-you-happier

David Steindl-Rast
www.gratefulness.org

Quilting resources
www.generations-quilt-patterns.com/quilt-guilds.html
www.quiltersguild.org.uk
www.quiltmuseum.org

academic studies

Many of these resources have been referred to during research for this book.

David DeSteno, Ye Li, Leah Dickens, and Jennifer S. Lerner, "Gratitude: A Tool for Reducing Economic Impatience," *Psychological Science* 25 (June 2014), 1262–67

Robert A. Emmons and M. E. McCullough, "Counting Blessings Versus Burdens: An Experimental Investigation of Gratitude and Subjective Well-being in Daily Life," *Journal of Personality and Social Psychology* 84/2 (2003), 377–89, www.psy.miami.edu/faculty/mmccullough/gratitude/Emmons_McCullough_2003_JPSP.pdf

Robert A. Emmons and M. E. McCullough, "Highlights from the Research Project on Gratitude and Thankfulness: Dimensions and Perspectives of Gratitude," Universities of California, Davis, and Miami, 2003, www.psy.miami.edu/faculty/mmccullough/Gratitude-Related%20Stuff/highlights_fall_2003.pdf

"The Gratitude Questionnaire Six-item Form," www.psy.miami.edu/faculty/mmccullough/gratitude/GQ-6-scoring-interp.pdf, from Michael E. McCullough, Robert A. Emmons, and Jo-Ann Tsang, "The Grateful Disposition: A Conceptual and Empirical Topography," *Journal of Personality and Social Psychology*, 82/1 (2002), 112–27, available at www.greatergood.berkeley.edu/pdfs/GratitudePDFs/7McCullough-GratefulDisposition.pdf

Laura E. Kurtz, and Sara B. Algoe, "Putting Laughter in Context: Shared Laughter as Behavioral Indicator of Relationship Well-being," *Personal Relationships* 22 (2015), 573–90, doi: 10.1111/pere.12095

Michael E. McCullough, Marcia B. Kimeldorf, and Adam D. Cohen, "An Adaptation for Altruism? The Social Causes, Social Effects, and Social Evolution of Gratitude," *Current Directions in Psychological Science* 17 (2008), 281–84, www.psy.miami.edu/faculty/mmccullough/Papers/Gratitude_CDPS_2008.pdf

Emily L. Polak and Michael E. McCullough, 'Is Gratitude an Alternative to Materialism?,' *Journal of Happiness Studies* 7 (2006), 343–60, www.psy.miami.edu/faculty/mmccullough/Papers/gratitude_materialism.pdf

Alexandra Sifferlin, "Why Being Thankful Is Good for You," *Time*, November 23, 2015, www.time.com/4124288/thanksgiving-day-2015-thankful-gratitude

University of North Carolina at Chapel Hill, "The Little Things: Gratitude and Shared Laughter Strengthen Romantic Partnerships," *Science Daily*, February 22, 2016, www.sciencedaily.com/releases/2016/02/160222144546.htm

index

acknowledgments

With grateful thanks to the highly creative team at CICO—particularly Carmel Edmonds, for approaching me to write about such a fabulous subject, and for her skilled editing. This is as much Carmel's book as it is mine. Many thanks also to Kristine Pidkameny for commissioning the book. Thank you, too, to those who have shared their stories, provided feedback, or have contributed in some way, including: the Burges family, the Revd Canon Andrew Haviland, Sue Hook, Bev James, Libby Jones, Karen Kain, Sue Lanson, Mary Lou Nash, Vanda "Joy" North, Audrey Paisey, Revd Mary Ridgewell, Dr Christina Volkmann, and Pat Watson. And, of course, thank you to my wonderful family, especially my father and Richard.